Twayne's United States Authors Series

Sylvia E. Bowman, *Editor*

INDIANA UNIVERSITY

T. S. Eliot

T. S. ELIOT

by PHILIP R. HEADINGS

University of Illinois

 57

Twayne Publishers, Inc.   ::   New York

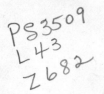

52857

MANUFACTURED IN THE UNITED STATES OF AMERICA BY
UNITED PRINTING SERVICES, INC.
NEW HAVEN, CONN.

To
LOIS AND BRIAN

Preface

BECAUSE THE NATURE and the stature of T. S. Eliot's poetry made inevitable the rapid accretion of a bewildering body of commentary and explication, the beginning student of Eliot finds himself faced with a confusing variety of interpretations and evaluations of the individual poems and plays. Many of these, of course, are excellent studies, some being extremely helpful to the novice and some to the specialist; many, however, tend to lead *away from* rather than *into* Eliot's art.

This mass of commentary has arisen chiefly because of two well-known characteristics of Eliot's poetry: its wide-ranging literary allusions and the fact that it is not chiefly by logical connections that the poems cohere. As to the latter, Eliot has remarked, "The chief use of the 'meaning' of a poem, in the ordinary sense, may be . . . to satisfy one habit of the reader, to keep his mind diverted and quiet, while the poem does its work upon him: much as the imaginary burglar is always provided with a bit of nice meat for the housedog."

The problems of "meaning" in the poetry, then, are not the most important ones. They are of such secondary nature that in *The Waste Land* and in some other poems Eliot has left out the logical meaning almost entirely, making it impossible for the reader to think he is experiencing the poem properly while missing the more important things—the peculiarly poetic things—that go on within the poem. I try, therefore, in this study to deal chiefly with the experiential content that *is* important in each of the works discussed. My intent is to sketch, in terms as simple as seem to me appropriate, the central schemes of the major works—hoping, meanwhile, that the reader will follow the discussion with the texts of the poems in mind or at hand.

Except in passing, I do not emphasize the metrical and dramatic techniques employed; nor do I pay more than sporadic and secondary attention to Eliot as critic. Instead, I place primary emphasis on the poems and plays themselves—their content and intentions, and the world-view implicit in them. I present them as poems and plays—not as riddles, puzzles, nor games. In general I make no attempt to trace sources and influences except as necessary in order to support readings that differ from those usually advanced. I also stress the unity of each work and the thematic consistency of the whole body of poetry studied.

I seek to demonstrate that the brief, lucid poem *Animula* constitutes for many readers a proper starting point for the study of Eliot's poems and plays—that the doctrine of the soul that it translates from Dante's near-translation of Aristotle is implicit in all of them; that the mythic method of *The Waste Land* throws much light on earlier and later works; and that the religious orientation of *Ash-Wednesday* is neither opposed to nor very different from that underlying such earlier poems as *Gerontion, The Waste Land,* and *The Hollow Men.*

I hope to show that Eliot's most difficult works are simpler and more unified than has often been thought and that his simplest and most accessible ones will reward re-readers with new and deeper insights. My chief aim is to approach the poems and plays on their own terms—to find the simple core of intent and focus for each major work and to read it from there.

Whether this book exaggerates the importance of Dante's influence on Eliot's works is for others to decide. But no one, I think, will deny that that influence is the most pervasive and, in most published studies, the least adequately interpreted one. Dante's influence far overshadows those of such writers as Bradley, St. John of the Cross, Laforgue, the Elizabethan playwrights, and the Metaphysical poets. Each of these is important at certain periods or in certain works, but the Dantean psychology and world-view, and especially the Dantean esthetique, remain central in Eliot's poetry from *The Love Song of J. Alfred Prufrock* to *The Elder Statesman.*

I am greatly indebted to Professors Francis Fergusson, Leonard Unger, Newton Stallknecht, Richard Ellmann, Roy Battenhouse, Roy Swanson, Horst Frenz, John Alford, Hubert Heffner, and especially Norbert Fuerst for my developing concern with the topics involved in this study and for much besides. I am further indebted in ways no longer possible to sort out to all those writers on Eliot cited in the selected bibliography and to many not cited. To Professor Sylvia Bowman I am grateful not only for excellent editorial criticism and advice, but also for the patient offices of friend and challenging teacher.

I am solely responsible for whatever deficiencies or errors may be found here. My greatest debt is acknowledged in the dedication.

PHILIP R. HEADINGS

The University of Illinois
Urbana, April 11, 1963

Acknowledgments

For permission to quote many passages from his works I am very grateful to Mr. T. S. Eliot and to his American and British publishers as follows:

To Harcourt, Brace & World, Inc., American publishers of *The Complete Poems and Plays 1909-1950; Selected Essays 1917-1932; The Rock;* and *The Confidential Clerk.* To Farrar, Straus & Company, Inc., American publishers of *The Elder Statesman* and *On Poetry and Poets.* To Faber and Faber, Ltd., publishers of all the above and *The Use of Poetry and the Use of Criticism.* To Barnes & Noble, Inc., and Methuen & Co., Ltd., publishers of *The Sacred Wood.*

I also wish to thank J. M. Dent & Sons, Ltd., Publishers and E. P. Dutton & Co., Inc., for permission to quote a number of passages from the Temple Classics bilingual editions of *The Divine Comedy* by Dante, English translation by J. A. Carlyle, Thomas Okey, and P. H. Wicksteed, and *La Vita Nuova* by Dante, English translation by Dante Gabriel Rossetti.

Finally, I wish to acknowledge my indebtedness to the Vedanta Society of Southern California and Phoenix House of London for permission to quote from *The Song of God*: *Bhagavad-Gita,* translated by Swami Prabhavananda and Christopher Isherwood, in the Mentor edition published by The New American Library (1954).

Contents

✗ 1905 - Read Rubaiyat of Omar Khayyam
First interest in poetry.

Chronology

Mid-   Andrew Eliot emigrated from East Coker, Somerset,
1600's   England, to Beverly, Massachusetts.

1834   The Reverend William Greenleaf Eliot graduated from
         Harvard; moved to St. Louis.

1888   September 26, Thomas Stearns Eliot was born.

1888-   Lived in St. Louis; spent summers in New England.
1905

1898-   Attended Smith Academy and Milton Academy; wrote
1906   "Byronic" first poems.

1906-   Harvard undergraduate and then graduate student
1910   (class of '09).

1910-   Paris year; studied at Sorbonne.
1911

1911-   Continued graduate studies at Harvard in philosophy;
1914   began friendship with Bertrand Russell.

1914   Traveling fellowship to Germany interrupted by World
         War I; settled in London (first at Oxford).

1914-   Close association with Ezra Pound, whose sponsorship
1922   led to Eliot's early successful publications and to various
         writing and editing assignments. Married Vivienne Haigh-
         Wood (1915), taught school, worked at Lloyds' Bank.

1922   Became editor of *The Criterion*. *The Waste Land* was
         published and won the $2000 Dial Award.

1925   Joined publishing firm of Faber and Gwyer, later Faber
         and Faber, of which he has since been a member.

1926   Clark Lecturer, Trinity College, Cambridge.

1927-   Became British citizen and member of Anglican Church.
1930   Wrote highly Dantean and overtly Christian poems and
         prose, including *Ash-Wednesday, Animula, Dante*.

1927-   First attempts at drama: *Sweeney Agonistes* and *The
1934   Rock*; "A Dialogue on Poetic Drama." Returned to
         America as Charles Eliot Norton Professor of Poetry,
         Harvard University, 1932-33.

1933- Honorary doctorates from eighteen leading American,
1959 British, and European universities.

1935- Major dramatic success: *Murder in the Cathedral*; first
1939 of the quartets: *Burnt Norton*; second major play: *The Family Reunion*. Discontinuance of *The Criterion* (1939).

1940- The three other quartets—all assured masterpieces—
1942 culminating in Eliot's *Paradiso* XXXIII: *Little Gidding*.

1943 President, Virgil Society. President, Classical Association.

1947 Death of Mrs. Eliot, after years of illness.

1948- Awarded Nobel Prize and the Order of Merit. Wrote
1949 most successful verse play of the twentieth century to date: *The Cocktail Party*.

1954 Hanseatic Goethe Prize.

1955 *The Confidential Clerk.*

1957 Married Valerie Fletcher.

1959 Eliot's *Oedipus at Colonus*: *The Elder Statesman*. Dante Gold Medal (Florence).

T. S. Eliot

CHAPTER 1

Significant Soil

HARDLY A POETRY READER is now alive who has not been becalmed and bemused in the yellow fog of *The Love Song of J. Alfred Prufrock,* the first of T. S. Eliot's poems to achieve publication beyond the environs of the schools attended by the poet. Prufrock, who memorably "measured out [his] life in coffee spoons," has often been mistaken for his author; but it is obvious, if for no other reason than the difference in their ages, that Prufrock was a constructed personality, a mask or persona, and that not only the poet but Prufrock as well was aware of the dry humor in his predicaments and his makeup.

Echoing a long tradition of dialogues between self and soul or heart and mind in Western poetry, the poem is a dialogue between "you and I," between the inner and outer or the private and public selves of a reticent middle-aged man who still has stirrings and aspirations outside the normal patterns of his civilized life, or rather outside the patterns of the polite society to which he is accustomed. He debates whether to try to break out of the mold, tries for the last time to disturb the universe by asking of a lady at a party "an overwhelming question." Finally he gives it up, saying "No! I am not Prince Hamlet, nor was meant to be; /Am an attendant lord, one that will do/To swell a progress, start a scene or two/. . . . I grow old . . ."

Though his reverie is heightened by allusions to *Hamlet* and to Dante's *Divine Comedy,* as well as to a number of other literary works, the poem is unmistakably modern in tone and diction. It combines and juxtaposes—as Eliot's poems were repeatedly to do—the remote and the familiar, the traditional and the contemporary; it mixes to good purpose not only memory and desire but also the grand and the deflated style.

We know at the end of the poem that Prufrock will continue to circulate in the drawing rooms where the women come and go, talking of Michelangelo, and that he will continue to measure out his life in coffee spoons—the common lot, presumably, of sophisticated human beings. The reader has seen the moment of Prufrock's greatness flicker, seen him give up the attempt and accept his almost amusing limitations: "I have heard the mermaids singing, each to each./I do not think that they will sing to me."

That poem of 1915 immediately earned for its author recognition as a writer with something new to say to his audience. After three slim volumes of poems had greatly extended his reputation, Eliot published in 1922 *The Waste Land,* a poem which many writers have called the most influential poem of the twentieth century. From such beginnings has grown what is perhaps the outstanding poetic and critical reputation in English and American letters of our time—notwithstanding the protests of a small but persistent and heated group of detractors who object chiefly to the "difficulty" of some of Eliot's poems and to the conservative, religious cast of his public personality and of some of his writings.

Eliot's insistence on preserving the privacy of his daily life has upset would-be purveyors of his fame, but the poet-playwright-critic has repeatedly stated that "there is no interest in the artist apart from his art" and that his works must speak for themselves. Nonetheless, the intensely personal nature of the poems themselves makes relevant a minimal amount of biography and also some consideration of the relations between the poet's life and times and the literary works which won for him in 1948 the Nobel Prize and the Order of Merit. The effect of his family background and personal history on his poems has been pointed out by Eliot himself on a number of occasions.

I *Personal Landscape*

Youngest of seven children in a St. Louis family of solid New England background, Thomas Stearns Eliot was born September 26, 1888. His ancestor Andrew Eliot (1627-1704) had emigrated in mid-life to Beverly, Massachusetts, from East Coker, a Somerset village in England, and later became town clerk and one of the jurors who tried the Salem witches. In 1834, the Reverend William Greenleaf Eliot, D.D., the grandfather of T. S. Eliot, graduated from Harvard and then moved to St. Louis, where he founded the first Unitarian church in that city. Later he founded Washington University and in 1872 became its chancellor. The family's ties with New England, however, were kept strong; and they formed, according to the poet, an important part of his early impressions. When in 1959 the American Academy of Arts and Sciences presented the Emerson-Thoreau Medal to Eliot for his achievement in literature, he told the New England assemblage that his childhood summers had been spent on the New England coast and the remaining seasons in drably urban St. Louis, so that his store of recurrent imagery included the Mississippi River and Massachusetts seashore and the St. Louis background modified later by that of London and Paris.[1] In this address Eliot was preparing his listeners for a reading of *The Dry Salvages*, but the two chief settings referred to—the city and the New England coast—have been used and imaged in much of his poetry.

In the Eliot family circle, there was great interest in literature, in other cultural matters, and in public service. The Unitarian faith of the family was qualified for Tom Eliot to some extent by the Catholic nurse who on at least one occasion took the young boy to her church service. In *American Literature and the American Language* Eliot stated his opinion of the value of his familial environment, which was governed by his grandfather's rules urging duty to the city, the church, and the university which he had founded. To Eliot such principles seemed excellent training for any child.[2]

II *Literary Influences*

Eliot has said that the writers of the recent past may give the beginning writer something to rebel against, and that for models such a writer may well go to remoter times, places, and languages. Much of his own early "originality," he says, consisted of attempts to transmute to his own time and place the purposes and accomplishments of such remote writers.[3]

His first excitement about poetry, he recalls,[4] came at fourteen when he picked up at home a copy of Fitzgerald's *The Rubaiyat of Omar Khayyam*. From 1898 to 1905, Eliot attended Smith Academy, which was associated with Washington University. He has called his years there the most important part of his education because particular emphasis was placed on what he considered the essentials: classical languages and history, English and American history, modern languages and mathematics.[5] By 1904, when he was sixteen, he had read Byron and had begun to write some poetry. The following year four of his poems appeared in the *Smith Academy Record*.[6] Eliot referred to them as "verses in the manner of *Don Juan*, tinged with that disillusion and cynicism only possible at the age of sixteen."[7]

He spent the 1905-1906 school year at Milton Academy in Massachusetts before entering Harvard in the fall of 1906. About this time he first read the poetry of John Donne. During his three undergraduate years at Harvard, nine of his poems, including the 1910 Class Ode, as well as editorials and reviews, appeared in the *Harvard Advocate*. Several of the poems showed the influence of Jules Laforgue, one result of a pivotal experience in the young poet's career: the reading, in 1908, of Arthur Symons' *The Symbolist Movement in Literature*. Until then, Eliot's poetry had been clearly derivative of his romantic predecessors in English poetry. In "The Perfect Critic" he later wrote: "But if we can recall the time when we were ignorant of the French symbolists, and met with *The Symbolist Movement in Literature*, we remember that book as an introduction to wholly new feelings, as a revelation. After we have read Verlaine and Laforgue and Rimbaud and return to Mr. Symons' book, we may find that our own impressions dissent from his. The book has not, perhaps, a permanent value for the one reader, but it has led to results of permanent importance for him."[8]

The nature of the influences derived from this reading is clarified in Eliot's 1950 lecture entitled "What Dante Means to Me": From Jules Laforgue, he says, he learned that his own speech idioms had poetic possibilities; from Baudelaire, that his urban experience could be material for poetry and that juxtaposing the realistic and the fantastic could produce striking effects.[9]

The chief marks of Laforgue's influence, which was to be quite important in the earlier published poems but to diminish markedly by 1920—though never, perhaps, to wholly disappear— were the sometimes bitter irony of tone and the rather cynical self-criticism of the personae or masks through whom the poems were spoken. So Prufrock was now equipped to ask, "Shall I say, I have gone at dusk through narrow streets/And watched the smoke that rises from the pipes/Of lonely men in shirt-sleeves, leaning out of windows . . ." and to answer, "No! I am not Prince Hamlet, nor was meant to be. . . ."[10] The young man of *Portrait of a Lady* could now long to "take the air, in a tobacco trance," and the similar personae of *Preludes, Rhapsody on a Windy Night, Morning at the Window,* and *Conversation Galante* could poetically experience or re-experience their observations of their own unreal but more deeply real cities—unreal in their difference from the traditional settings of art, but real as moral and esthetic experience.

Such symbolist influences, of course, were added to Eliot's earlier patterns and interests. Moreover, the most important influence from this period—that of Dante—we have not yet mentioned. Some forty years later in tracing Dante's influence back to about 1910, Eliot termed it, "The most persistent and deepest influence upon my own verse." This influence, which we will examine specifically in Chapter 2 and recurrently throughout the book, provided the psychology and the moral perspective for the personae through whom Eliot's Laforguian irony was to address their Baudelairean cities.

Eliot's persona technique in *Prufrock* doubtless owed something to Ezra Pound and William Butler Yeats. Many years later Eliot wrote that when he first read Pound's *Personae* and *Exultations* in 1910, he was too involved with Laforgue to be excited by them, but that he did find Pound's more interesting than any other contemporary poems he had found.

III *Personae*

It is noteworthy that Eliot links in the above quotation the names of Pound and Yeats, two of the most eminent practitioners of what had already by 1915 become in his own poems a characteristic technique: the construction of an at least partly fictitious identity through whom a poem is spoken. The word "personae" was of course no more the invention of Pound than was the tactic to which it refers, and he laid no claim to either; but the term achieved much greater currency in criticism after he used it as the title of his 1909 collection of poems. Eliot's Prufrock, in 1911, spoke of "prepar[ing] a face to meet the faces that you meet," a reasonably accurate description of the author's creation of Prufrock as the mask or persona through whom his poem would be spoken. Both Pound and Eliot used the technique with great subtlety and effectiveness in their prose as well as in their poems.

The playwright, of course, constantly speaks through the personae that he has created, and hence the danger of taking any speech from a play as the unvarnished opinion of the author. For example, we can hardly call the speeches of Hamlet and Antony more the views of Shakespeare than those of Polonius and

Enobarbus—at least not without carefully considering the entire dramatic situations in which those characters appear. Similarly, much of the misinterpretation of the works of Eliot and of Pound arises from the failure of the reader to grasp, in a given poem, both the identity of the persona used and the distinction between the intentions and perceptions of the persona and those of the author.

Most of Eliot's poems, in fact almost all of those preceding *Ash-Wednesday* (1930), are thus organized in the consciousness and semi-consciousness of male personae who comment on their environments, often ironically but usually with genuine compassion. What the reader must intuit for each poem is the identity of its organizing persona and the quality and direction of his experience. The short early poem *Morning at the Window* may serve to illustrate:

> They are rattling breakfast plates in basement kitchens,
> And along the trampled edges of the street
> I am aware of the damp souls of housemaids
> Sprouting despondently at area gates.
>
> The brown waves of fog toss up to me
> Twisted faces from the bottom of the street,
> And tear from a passer-by with muddy skirts
> An aimless smile that hovers in the air
> And vanishes along the level of the roofs.[11]

The reader's task is to identify with the "I" of the third line—the man looking down from a window at the waking but unattractive environment that twists not only the faces but also the souls of the people he sees below. In the words and rhythm of the first line the reader hears the rattling of the plates and the flat conversation that crosses the breakfast tables. The "trampled edges of the street" testify to the number of aimless, uninterested, and uninteresting existences passed on this street.

But the deepest significance lies in the attitude of the observer toward the lives of this street, both his own and those he sees in distorted snatches. Behind "the damp souls" he senses what Eliot called in *Preludes* "The notion of some infinitely gentle/Infinitely suffering thing." And in the words "damp," "twisted," and "aimless," he implies that these people deserve a more significant existence involving a scheme of moral order. In this poem and couched in completely secular terms is a doctrine of individual worth and of human sympathy and acceptance of responsibility. (The "I" did not just wipe his hand across his mouth and laugh as is ironically suggested to the reader of the earlier *Preludes.*)

In similar fashion all of Eliot's poems and plays were to speak of experience common to men of most faiths, even though that experience would sometimes (most exclusively in *The Rock, Ash-Wednesday,* and *Murder in the Cathedral*) be expressed in the terminology of Christianity which permeates the Western cultural tradition; sometimes in the terminology of other religions (often of several in the same poem); and sometimes, as in this poem, in wholly secular terms. The mixing or counterpointing of religious and secular symbols is as characteristic of the *Four Quartets* and of the late plays as of *The Waste Land* and other earlier poems. In this respect, as in many others, Eliot followed the example of Dante.

Just as in *Morning at the Window,* we see in most of Eliot's poems, early and late, a persona, a male protagonist or organizing consciousness who watches around him the ravages of improperly ordered love (sometimes his own) and who raises questions of justice and injustice, of merit or blame, of the responsibility of the watchers (including himself and the reader) implied in the scenes and souls depicted. Such figures are seen in Prufrock, who comments on his own unheroic destiny; in the young man of *Portrait of a Lady,* sitting on a park bench reading his newspaper and observing self-possessedly the life of his city; in the observer of *Preludes,* who combines male with female insights into the malady of his city; in the suffering witness of *Rhapsody on a Windy Night,* who regards the prostitute framed in the light of a door, the "automatic hand" of a child, and the moon which has lost its memory; in the critically aware "I" who hands the Boston *Evening Transcript* to Cousin Harriet; in the detached observer who retrospectively links the submarine laughter of *Mr. Apollinax* with Phlebas the Phoenician, Homer's Old Man of the Sea, and Rimbaud's *Le Bateau Ivre* through the lines "Hidden under coral islands/Where worried bodies of drowned men drift down in the green silence, /Dropping from fingers of surf"; and in the observer of the desertion in *La Figlia che Piange.* Such a figure, especially, is the poet who organizes his observations of the ravages of lust in its leading forms in *Burbank with a Baedeker* . . . , in *Sweeney Erect,* and in *Sweeney Among the Nightingales.* The most impressive instance of such intent and usage is seen in *The Waste Land,* of which more will be said in Chapter 4. Certainly Pound's influence on Eliot's adaptation of the technique was considerable, beginning as early as his 1910 reading of Pound.

IV   *Europe or America?*

Concluding his baccalaureate degree in 1909, Eliot went on to graduate school, concentrating his studies in philosophy and logic. In 1910 he received the Master of Arts degree; the next year was spent in Paris, where he attended the Sorbonne, reading chiefly French literature and philosophy. Here he was tutored by Alain-Fournier and attended the lectures of Henri Bergson, which he later described as extremely impressive. He read Claudel, André Gide, and Dostoyevsky, and also a book figuring in several of his poems—*Bubu of Montparnasse.* After his study in Paris, he visited Munich, where in 1911 he finished that first famous poem, *The Love Song of J. Alfred Prufrock*, begun at Harvard in 1910 and later dedicated to the poet Jean Verdenal, a friend of his Paris year.

It seems probable that by this time *Conversation Galante, Portrait of a Lady*, and *Preludes* I and II had been written. *Conversation Galante*, which has been called the most Laforguian of Eliot's poems, is a self-consciously witty dialogue, a playful sparring match between a young male protagonist and the young lady with whom he is walking. Its exhausting gaiety has a pathetic quality, and its explicit irony is doubled by another implicit level of irony.

The title *Portrait of a Lady* suggests Henry James's novel of the same name and Ezra Pound's poem *Portrait d'une Femme,* a more proximate source. More accurately Eliot's poem might be called a portrait of a young man; for, through his examinations and re-examinations of himself and the lady, we become intimately acquainted with the somewhat tortured protagonist whose youth may or may not eventuate in the poignant anticlimax of Prufrock's middle age, but seems unlikely to lead to the bored dissatisfaction of the lady herself.

In the fall of 1911, at the age of twenty-three, Eliot returned to Harvard and studied, under Professor Josiah Royce, the epistemological systems of Meinong and Bradley. He was also occupied with Sanskrit, Pali, and the metaphysics of Patanjali. Although several poems were written during this time, no writing of Eliot's was published between 1910 and 1915. It was probably in 1911 that *Preludes* III and IV, *Rhapsody on a Windy Night*, and *La Figlia che Piange* were completed.

The *Preludes* give observations and meditations on loneliness in a city, from a less personally oriented perspective than those of *Portrait of a Lady* and *Rhapsody on a Windy Night*. The four sections of the poem present images—sights, sounds, smells, and inner tensions—all of which mirror back the "notion of some infinitely gentle, infinitely suffering thing," the human soul. Last, the poet looks at himself and his empathy and sardonically adds "Wipe your hand across your mouth and laugh;/The worlds revolve like ancient women gathering fuel in vacant lots."

In *Rhapsody on a Windy Night* the young man walks through the streets at twelve o'clock, half past one, half past two, half past three, and four o'clock in the morning. He is searching for some essence or experience which comes at him or looms at him obliquely but never appears—searching for what in the nature of things, as *Gerontion* later explained, he could not allow himself, even if it were offered. The genuine desperation of the poem comes through its language convincingly; the scene might almost come from Dante's *Inferno*.

La Figlia che Piange makes of a described parting of lovers something of a Joycian epiphany—a recreated moment of dawning moral awareness. The protagonist pretends to have been only an observer, but his deep involvement in the scene makes the reader feel that the narrator was a participant. He sees himself as the mind of an artist, and he regards the girl as a body torn and bruised. And the parting is described as resembling the mind's desertion of the body it has used. The poem contains strong echoes of Sestina XI in Dante's *Vita Nuova*, of Rossetti's *Blessed Damozel*, and of the end of Conrad's *Heart of Darkness*. The protagonist tries to use artistic significance as justification for the desertion, but he has not wholly succeeded in convincing himself, let alone the reader.

For the 1913-14 school year Eliot was appointed an assistant in philosophy, and indeed philosophy seems during this period to have received most of his attention. While an assistant, he met and studied with Bertrand Russell, then a visiting lecturer and the probable model of the poem *Mr. Apollinax*. In this poem the subdued and sophisticated faculty-tea atmosphere is splintered by a foreign visitor, whose Apollonian depth and Protean vitality drown out for the observing protagonist all memory of the hosts and hostesses except "a slice of lemon and a bitten macaroon." Russell was quite impressed by Eliot's abilities, and their friendship was later to be important to the young poet when he was an expatriate in London.

We may be sure that the urge to live and write in Europe had been alive and growing for some time. As Kristian Smidt writes:

> The notion of settling there [in England] was not strange to him. As early as 1909, recognizing "the failure of American life" at that time, he wrote [*Harvard Advocate*, May 7, 1909] in a book review of the class of "Americans retained to their native country by business relations or socialities or by a sense of duty—the last reason implying a real sacrifice—while their hearts are always in Europe." Henry James was a Londoner, and was soon to become a British subject; Pound, J. G. Fletcher, Aiken, H. D. [Hilda Doolittle], and Robert Frost all lived in England in the years preceding and during the Great War. And Mr. Tinckom-Fernandez tells us that while at college he and Eliot discussed the idea of emigrating to a milieu more congenial to a writer, as Ezra Pound had done. When Tinckom-Fernandez did go to Europe, Eliot saw him off.[12]

Having been awarded a traveling fellowship for the 1914-15 year, Eliot spent some weeks of the summer in Germany, chiefly at Marburg. The start of World War I at the end of the summer, however, changed his traveling plans, and he went to Merton College at Oxford in September. There he read Greek philosophy, the German phenomenologists Meinong and Husserl, and, "above all" (says Kristian Smidt), Aristotle. Eliot's interest in Aristotle was to be continually compounded and extended as it blended with his deep involvement in Dante.

Whether by chance or design, Eliot's stay in England was to become permanent. It would be 1932 before he saw America again, and by then he had become a British subject. In London, in 1914, he lived in the neighborhood of Russell Square, the setting of the brief poem *Morning at the Window*. And on September 22, 1914, through his friend and classmate Conrad Aiken, he met Ezra Pound, who was to have a profound influence on his career and his poetry, especially during the next eight years.

V *Pound and Publication*

Of the numerous influences on Eliot's poetic career, none was to be more important than that of Ezra Pound, which came at a crucial period. Eliot's early education, his Harvard background, and his interests had already sent him along the paths Pound was advocating with his typical verve and impatience. If Pound's influence, therefore, was not germinal, it did strongly reinforce tendencies already apparent in Eliot before their meeting in 1914. By this time he had written not only his *Smith Academy Review* and *Harvard Advocate* poems, but also most of those to be published through Pound's influence and connections within the succeeding three-year period, culminating in the volume *Prufrock and Other Observations* of 1917.

Of Pound's influence Eliot has written: "My indebtedness to Pound is of two kinds: first, in my literary criticism; . . . second, in his criticism of my poetry in our talk, and his indications of desirable territories to explore. This indebtedness extends from 1915 to 1922, after which period Mr. Pound left England, and our meetings became infrequent."[13]

Pound called Eliot, soon after their first meeting, "the only American I know of who has made what I can call adequate preparation for writing. He has actually trained himself *and* modernized himself *on his own*. . . . It is such a comfort to meet a man and not have to tell him to wash his face, wipe his feet, and remember the date (1914) on the calendar."[14] Moreover, the two poets were voluntary expatriates for similar reasons. Pound wrote in 1914, "London may not be the Paradiso Terrestrae, but it is at least some centuries nearer it than is St. Louis."[15]

Conrad Aiken had tried for some time to help find a publisher for some of Eliot's poems, but without success; Pound was now to fare better, but not without a struggle. Of the poems that Eliot showed him, he picked out *Prufrock* as the one surest to succeed and to mark its author as different from any other poet then writing. After a prolonged campaign, Pound finally persuaded or perhaps bludgeoned Harriet Monroe, editor of *Poetry* (Pound was a contributing editor), into printing the poem. He had evidently suggested some changes in the poem, since he wrote Miss Monroe regarding the Hamlet passage, "It is an early and choice bit and T. E. won't give it up, and as it is the only portion of the poem that most readers will like at first reading, I don't see that it will do much harm."[16]

After the impression created by *Prufrock*, Pound had less difficulty in helping, during 1915, to place a number of Eliot's other poems in *Poetry*, in Wyndham Lewis' effervescent periodical *Blast*, and in *Others*. He seems also to have been instrumental in Eliot's appointment as an assistant editor of the *Egoist* in 1917. And Pound himself published five of Eliot's poems in his *Catholic Anthology*—the first appearance in book form of any of Eliot's verse.[17]

The "programs" of Eliot and Pound dovetailed at a number of points, despite their marked differences in temperament. Each felt strongly about the value of tradition and the necessity of discipline in poetry; each considered Dante perhaps the greatest of poets and the finest model for a beginning poet to study. Eliot had already deeply immersed himself in Dante, studying and memorizing many passages from the Temple Classics bilingual edition. As he later said in the preface to his 1929 book, *Dante,* after acknowledging the influence of the *Dante* of Professor Charles Grandgent of Harvard, "I owe something to an essay by Mr. Ezra Pound in his *Spirit of Romance,* but more to his table-talk; and I owe something to Mr. Santayana's essay in *Three Philosophical Poets.*"[18]

Perhaps one of Pound's chief influences on Eliot's interest in Dante was to turn his attention to the Arnaut Daniel passage in Provençal (the only sustained passage in which Dante allowed one of his characters to speak in a tongue other than Dante's own)—the passage that Eliot was to cite and use so often in his later writings. Though even that interest may have preceded their acquaintance, it was very likely Pound's vigorous sounding of Arnaut Daniel's speech that impressed Eliot so deeply with it.

Certainly Pound's swashbuckling and uninhibited attempts to "educate the heathens" must have excited and appealed to the milder, more decorous younger poet (Eliot was twenty-six and Pound thirty in 1915). On one occasion, when Eliot tried in a poem to copy his friend's free-wheeling tactics, Pound admonished him, "That's not your style at all. You let *me* throw the bricks through the front window. You go in at the back door and take out the swag."[19]

Through Pound, Eliot became acquainted with many of the writers and artists who were to shape the thinking of their era, not a few of whom were kept inspired and even alive largely through the encouragement and assistance of the resourceful and energetic Pound. The list of artists who owed much to him before and during the 1920's is most impressive: Yeats, Joyce, Wyndham Lewis, the sculptor Gaudier-Brzeska, and Eliot, among others.

During the next year or two after meeting Pound, Eliot began writing reviews for philosophical journals; and he also completed his thesis, *Experience and the Objects of Knowledge in the Philosophy of F. H. Bradley* (not published until 1964), though he did not return to Harvard to take the examinations for his doctoral degree after the thesis had been accepted.

The young poet-philosopher, however, was hardly lost in books and study: On June 26, 1915, he married Vivienne Haigh-Wood, a ballet dancer and daughter of the painter Charles Haigh-Wood. He taught at High Wycombe Grammar School and then at the Highgate School for four terms. Part of this time the Eliots lived with Mrs. Eliot's parents in Hampstead and with Bertrand Russell in his London flat.

During the same period Eliot continued writing poetry, some of it in French; suffered the considerable financial difficulties likely at that time (according to Pound) to be the lot of anyone devoting himself to the arts; and finally took employment with Lloyds' Bank, where he was soon highly regarded. He remained there until, in 1925, he joined the publishing firm of Faber and Gwyer, later Faber and Faber, with which he has continued to be associated.

He also did extension lecturing, editorial work, and a great deal of reviewing and writing for periodicals. Overwork was very probably responsible for the poor health that in 1918, says F. O. Matthiessen,[20] kept him out of the United States Navy. Eliot was an editor of the *Egoist* from 1917 to 1919, and he was also listed on the editorial committee for *Coterie* in 1919, along with Richard Aldington, Aldous Huxley, and Wyndham Lewis. In 1922, he undertook the editorship of *The Criterion*—which position he held until discontinuance of publication in 1939—and he built for it a reputation of unusual distinction. As an outgrowth of his friendship with John Middleton Murry, Eliot contributed numerous articles and reviews to the *Athenaeum*, which Murry edited from 1919 to 1921.

The October 1922 issue of *The Criterion* contained what was to become the most controversial and the most influential poem of the first half of the twentieth century: Eliot's *The Waste Land*. Published correspondence between Eliot and Pound testifies to the "midwifery" of Pound in blue-penciling to about half its length the original manuscript. But at just this time Pound was leaving England for Paris, and the close association of the two poets was coming to an end.

The spirit of camaraderie that grew up between Pound and

Eliot and the depth of their mutual poetic concerns, as well as the lapse in rapport which soon caused their paths to diverge, may perhaps be foreseen behind the personae of Eliot's brief prose selection "Eeldrop and Appleplex," which appeared in two 1917 issues of *The Little Review*. Eeldrop, a bank clerk, a skeptic with a taste for mysticism, and Appleplex, a materialist with a leaning toward skepticism who studies the physical and biological sciences, repair from time to time to rooms in an "evil" neighborhood to study first-hand[21] the closest approximations to tragedy available since orthodox theology and its "admirable theory of the soul" have gone out of fashion. Both concerned over the "awful importance" of any ruined life,[22] the two of them formulate a definition of the artist that provides a tentative bridge between differing viewpoints, but not a conclusive agreement. They part on a note of slight embarrassment.

We must agree, however, when Eeldrop says that we are interested not in the artist but in his work,[23] and we must also remember that Eeldrop and Appleplex are not persons, but personae. And the similarity of "Appleplex" to "Apollinax" further clouds any argument for definitely linking Pound, rather than Russell, to the Appleplex persona. But his path and Eliot's did diverge. Eliot wrote in 1950, "There did come a point, of course, at which difference of outlook and belief became too wide; or it may have been distance and different environment, or it may have been both."[24]

Even after Pound moved to Paris in 1922 and the two saw each other much less frequently, great mutual respect for poetic abilities and accomplishments has survived many differences in viewpoint and the passage of forty years—hectic years for Pound in which his attacks on what he disapproved became more and more violent and sometimes aberrant. At least twenty of the items in Donald Gallup's excellent bibliography concern Eliot's writings on Pound, and Eliot is far from alone in his estimate of Pound as one of the most capable poets of the twentieth century: In 1949 Pound was awarded the Bollingen-Library of Congress Award for the best poetry by an American citizen published during the previous year (his *Pisan Cantos*). Without their association, especially during the period from 1915 to 1922, Eliot's life and poetic career might have been far different.

CHAPTER 2

Dante's Logic of the Sensibility:
The Simple Soul

ELIOT REMARKED in 1920, in *The Sacred Wood,* that Dante's *Divine Comedy* is "in some way a 'moral education,'"[1] and later, in his 1929 book, *Dante,* that "Dante has to educate our senses as he goes along."[2] Throughout his poetic career, Eliot has set those same tasks for himself, and he has used in his works "the logic of sensibility" that he took largely from Dante. Hence a number of his remarks on Dante are the most helpful available guides to Eliot's work:

> The effect of many books about Dante is to give the impression that it is more necessary to read about him than to read what he has written. But the next step after reading Dante again and again should be to read some of the books that he read, rather than modern books about his work and life and times, however good. . . . With Dante there is just as much need for concentrating on the text [as with Shakespeare], and all the more because Dante's mind is more remote from the ways of thinking and feeling in which we have been brought up. . . . the forms of imagination, phantasmagoria, and sensibility . . . [are] strange to us. We have to learn to accept these forms.[3]

Similarly, the reader of Eliot's poems who senses "the forms of imagination, phantasmagoria, and sensibility" at work in them will find implied the locus from which each poem can be read. And only then will it be profitable to attempt tracing the chronologically developing intentions and assumptions of the author, or even to evaluate any one of the poems in the proper terms.

Eliot's works often echo Dante's forms, techniques, subject matter, or even exact words. Like Dante himself, Eliot is a writer steeped in the Western cultural and literary tradition. Both his creative and critical works have echoed a wide range of authors—most importantly Shakespeare, Greek and Elizabethan dramatic poets, the Metaphysical and Symbolist poets, and the great philosophical poets of the Western tradition. Even in his earliest prose volume, *The Sacred Wood* (1920), he wrote on— besides Dante and other topics—Euripides, Christopher Marlowe, *Hamlet*, Ben Jonson, Philip Massinger, Swinburne, and Blake.

But for reasons already apparent in the 1920 "Dante" essay, no other writer was to assume such a central position in the whole body of Eliot's poetry as the Florentine exile. Dante's *Divine Comedy* familiarizes its reader with the path by which the earliest intimations of immortality and of felicity in a child-hood love become transmuted to the boundless felicity of the highest love, "redeeming the time" (*Ash-Wednesday*) that passes between. As in Dante's masterpiece, the experience of that path is the central theme of Eliot's poetry from *The Love Song of J. Alfred Prufrock* to the end of *Four Quartets*. From the beginning, Eliot has repeatedly emphasized this relevance of Dante to his poems.

Already we have seen tendencies that were to remain central in both Eliot's poems and plays throughout his career. Charac-teristically, a male persona with deep sympathy for his fellow men and a strong sense of moral and social responsibility examines the lives around him and raises "overwhelming" ques-tions. Eliot has early and late proclaimed his emulation of Dante in these respects and others, but the unmistakably explicit poetic expression of that indebtedness and of the doctrine of the soul at its center did not come until the publication in 1929 of *Animula* and of the *Dante* book, in which Eliot quoted in English and Italian the *Purgatorio* passage on which *Animula* was based and clearly set down his attitudes toward and debts to Dante. Though many strong links tie *Animula* to *Ash-Wednesday* and other writings of the same period, the assump-tions to which it gives clear statement had been implicit in Eliot's poetry as early as *Prufrock*. No other clues are as relevant to the reading of the entire body of Eliot's poetry.

Animula comprises not only a restatement of Dante's theory of the soul—his basic psychology, which Eliot calls "Aristotle's *De anima* strained through the Schools"—but also the clear statement of the psychology and philosophy basic to all of Eliot's major poetry. *Animula* assumes and defines the attitudes toward the human soul, free will, and individual responsibility implicit in the poetry of both poets; it is therefore one of the best starting points for a study of Eliot. The poem is based on *Purgatorio* XVI, in which Marco Lombardo answers Dante's questions about freedom of the will and about the nature of the soul. Eliot quotes the speech as follows:

> From the hands of Him who loves her before she is, there issues like a little child that plays, with weeping and laughter, the simple soul, that knows nothing except that, come from the hands of a glad creator, she turns willingly to everything that delights her. First she tastes the flavour of a trifling good; then is beguiled, and pursues it, if neither guide nor check withhold her. Therefore laws were needed as a curb; a ruler was needed, who should at least see afar the tower of the true city.[4]

F. O. Matthiessen cites this passage as an example of Dante's ability to "use the most concrete imagery as a 'means of making the spiritual visible,' "[5] and Eliot no doubt selected it for such reasons. Hence Eliot's recurrent praise of the Metaphysical poets and of all other writers who can make the reader experience an idea as immediately "as the odor of a rose."[6]

Eliot's adaptation of this passage in *Animula* falls into three quite distinctive parts: The first one, beginning, " 'Issues from the hand of God, the simple soul'/To a flat world of changing lights and noise,/To light, dark, dry or damp, chilly or warm" gives us the same concept of the soul and the love or *eros* that motivates it as is seen in Dante and in Aristotle's *De anima*. Eliot later showed this same picture of the soul of a child in *The Cultivation of Christmas Trees* (1956), and we might speculate that the poet restated this theme because its importance in interpreting his works had been too often overlooked.

The simple soul is seen as molded by its choices and by its environment; it builds its own Karma. It "confounds the actual and the fanciful," and

> The heavy burden of the growing soul
> Perplexes and offends more, day by day;
>
> . . . .
>
> The pain of living and the drug of dreams
> Curl up the small soul in the window seat
> Behind the *Encyclopaedia Britannica*.

This picture, drawn in the first twenty-three lines, is then restated in the next eight lines, beginning with an echoing of the first line of the poem (my italics):

> Issues from the hand of *time* the simple soul
> Irresolute and selfish, misshapen, lame,
> Unable to fare forward or retreat,
> Fearing the warm reality, the offered good,
>
> . . . .
>
> Living first in the silence after the viaticum.

The third and last section consists of six lines, a plea for prayer. The person addressed, who may be the reader or, more likely, the Virgin Mary, is asked to pray for a variety of persons whose lives were lost in various ways—who issued from the "hand of time" variously misshapen.

The tone and mood of this poem are akin to those of *Marina*; each of them displays an unguarded honesty, a humility and an acceptance of one's own limitations that are rarely encountered. The role assumed by the author is that of moral guide, directing the attention of the reader to those considerations which may help him to understand better his own psychic development and to accept the responsibility for exercising the proper choices, for using his free will in the proper directions, for acting rather than letting life slip away unprofitably, and for making for himself, through proper choice, the environment that will make possible further and better choices.

Yet, like Dante, Eliot acknowledges the great possibility that all will not turn out well and that some divine intervention, some good fortune beyond the influence of the individual, must intervene in time (soon enough) and in Time (not eternity) if all is to turn out well. It is worth noting the psychic foci of the persons prayed for in this third part of *Animula*. One lusted after speed and power; one, blown to pieces, was evidently intriguing or dealing in violence [World War I?]; one made a great fortune—satisfied his greed; one went his own way; and Floret, like Acteon, was slain by the boarhound for his lust.

The last line, borrowed (after Dante) from the "Hail Mary"—but with a twist—has a dual meaning that has been noted by various commentators: prayer is requested at "the hour of our birth"; first, the hour of physical birth, lest the simple soul should issue from the "hand of time" "irresolute and selfish, misshapen, lame." But the birth is not only physical birth: It may also be the obverse side of the coin of physical death, the entry to "the silence after the viaticum," the moment of truth when the soul knows its direction and understands its path, according to the doctrine explained to Dante in Canto XXV of *Purgatorio* by Statius, who adds the Christian dimension to Virgil's knowledge of the soul:

> When Lachesis has no more flax to twine,
>> It quits the flesh, but bears essentially
>> Away with it the human and divine—
> Each lower power in dumb passivity,
>> But memory, intelligence, and will
>> Active, and keener than they used to be.
> All of itself, as by a miracle,
>> Instant it lights on one or other shore;
>> Then first it knows its ways, for good or ill.[7]

This Christian version agrees also with the doctrines of the *Bhagavad-Gita*, which are also pervasively relevant to Eliot's poems and plays.

Dante's Virgil, not trusting his pupil to grasp wholly the significance of or even his first explanation of the nature of the soul's motives and movements, echoes the matter of the "simple soul" passage shortly afterward, explaining the arrangement of purgatory by reference to proper love and the several sorts of improper love.

Dante the Pilgrim asks him, "therefore I pray thee, sweet Father dear, that/thou define love to me, to which thou dost/ reduce every good work and its opposite."[8] Virgil replies by explaining that

> The mind which is created quick to love, is
>> responsive to everything that is pleasing, soon
>> as by pleasure it is awakened into activity.
> Your apprehensive faculty draws an impression
>> from a real object, and unfolds it within you,
>> so that it makes the mind turn thereto.
> And if, being turned, it inclines towards it, that
>> inclination is love; that is nature, which
>> through pleasure is bound anew within you.
> Then, even as fire moves upward by reason of
>> its form, whose nature it is to ascend, there
>> where it endures longest in its material;
> So the enamoured mind falls to desire, which is
>> a spiritual movement, and never rests until the
>> object of its love makes it rejoice.[9]

Dante understands, but he has further questions. He wants to know how, if "the soul walks with no other foot"—if, in other words, the soul cannot help loving and moving toward what draws its attention (as Freud would have it)[10]—can man merit reward or blame for his actions? And Virgil goes on to explain both man's instincts toward the highest good and his conscience, the innate "virtue which giveth counsel, and ought to guard the threshold of assent," so that man can either accept or reject an impulse of love; and it is in this guardianship of the threshold of assent that praise or blame is earned.[11] He says,

> Wherefore, suppose that every love which is
> kindled within you arises of necessity, the
> power to arrest it is within you.
> By the noble virtue Beatrice understands Freewill,
> and therefore, look that thou have this in mind,
> if she betake her to speak with thee thereof.[12]

In this passage of Dante, as in Aristotle and Plato before him, we see love (*eros, amor*) as the final cause or prime mover not only of the motions of a man's soul, but also of the entire universe.[13]

Here then is the doctrine of the soul, of volition and free will, and of individual responsibility for one's destiny which is the central psychology of Dante's *Divine Comedy*. And since, by this philosophy, the highest form of love comprises man's only proper activity, the ordering of love—of Plato and Aristotle's *eros*—is seen as man's highest calling and as the proper subject matter for his meditations, his speculations, and his art. To make the proper choices is man's highest privilege and his duty, and the improper choices are always those of loving the wrong things or of loving lesser things too much or greater ones too little. In order that the proper choices may be made, "Pray for us now and at the hour of our birth."

This doctrine of moral responsibility forms the deepest theme of most of Eliot's poetry and all of his plays, and it is those other authors and writings that deal with such questions best that Eliot most frequently quotes or alludes to in his art and his criticism: Dante, Shakespeare, the Bible, St. John of the Cross and other Christian mystics, the *Bhagavad-Gita*, the Greek dramatists, Baudelaire, and Christian ritual. Improper choices are the chief failures of Prufrock, the wastelanders, the hollow men, and of the unsuccessful characters in Eliot's plays. The proper choices, obversely, are the great triumphs of Dante's

Arnaut Daniel (quoted in *The Waste Land*), the protagonists of *Ash-Wednesday* and the *Four Quartets,* Thomas in *Murder in the Cathedral,* Harry in *The Family Reunion,* everyone except (for the time, at least) Peter Quilpe in *The Cocktail Party,* and most of the characters in *The Confidential Clerk* and in *The Elder Statesman.* In fact, for Eliot as for Dante, it might be said that the essential requirement of Comedy is that the important characters (or rather the leading characters; all are important) learn to make those choices which direct their psychic movements toward higher loves.

Epigraphs, borrowings from, and allusions to Dante have appeared frequently and consistently in Eliot's poems and plays from the Guido of Montefeltro epigraph of the 1911 *Prufrock* to the verb "transhumanize," translated from Dante in both *The Cocktail Party* and *The Elder Statesman,* in which, as Henri Fluchère points out, human love is seen as related to divine love and as the way to purgation and communion. Many references to Dante as a critical standard may also be found scattered throughout the body of Eliot's prose works. And the unity of *The Waste Land* can hardly be grasped without understanding the function of the Dante quotations and allusions contained in it.

In a talk on Dante in 1950, Eliot classed Dante with Shakespeare, Homer, and Virgil as one of the great masters to whom one slowly grows up, and added that after forty years, Dante still seemed to him the deepest and most lasting influence on his own poetry. He pointed out that he has borrowed lines from Dante, that he has set echoes of Dante in parallel to modern scenes for purposes of contrast and comparison, and that he has consciously imitated Dante in the air raid scene of *Little Gidding,* which cost him more trouble than any other passage of similar length that he has written. That section, incidentally, has frequently been called Eliot's best poetry.

He goes on to discuss three chief influences, which he sums up as the lessons of *craft,* of *speech,* and of *exploration of sensibility.* Of the first, the lesson of craft, he says that no poet of similar stature has been a more attentive student to the art of poetry than Dante. The second lesson taught by Dante's poetry —that of speech—is that as poet one should be the servant of his language rather than the master of it. He should refine and develop his language for those who come after him, which is the highest possible achievement of the poet's craft. This "purifying of the dialect of the tribe" has received Eliot's repeated attention at least since 1917 ("Tradition and the Individual Talent").

The great poet, Eliot says, should not be content to see and hear more clearly than ordinary men, but should perceive more than they and help them too to perceive it. The *Divine Comedy,* he says, expresses the full range of man's emotional possibilities, from despair to beatitude; it reminds later poets that they must similarly push back the frontiers of man's awareness.

Eliot's works characteristically attempt, with considerable success, to express the almost inexpressible: the self-probings of many of his personae, the dawning moral awareness of Sweeney, the moral and spiritual struggles of Thomas in *Murder in the Cathedral* and of *Ash-Wednesday,* and the search for one's proper place in the universe in all of the major works.

In Florence to receive the Dante Medal in 1959, Eliot said he did not feel that he deserved it; he admitted, however, that he could not think of anyone who did. The judgment might appropriately be left to readers of the "familiar compound ghost" section of *Little Gidding,* in which Dante's lessons of craft, of speech, and of exploration of sensibility are put to use.

CHAPTER 3

Another Country

BETWEEN THE PARIS YEAR (1910-11) and Eliot's departure for what was to be a permanent home in England (1914), we may be sure that a final reassessment of attitude toward the question of residence as an artist in the United States or in Europe took shape. In the poems of about 1915, such evaluations are clearly apparent. The nine lines of *The Boston Evening Transcript* contrast, for example, the protagonist and his awakening appetites of life with his staid Cousin Harriet, who sits at home and reads the *Transcript* and is swayed in its winds of opinion like a field of ripe corn. *Aunt Helen* similarly contrasts a maiden aunt, who lacks or suppresses the appetites of life, with her servants and the on-going life of the world not subject to her controls. In *Cousin Nancy*, the title character is a member of the younger American generation. She dances, smokes, and does the other modern things, while her aunts are uncertain whether or not to disapprove. Less undecided in their evaluations are "Matthew and Waldo, guardians of the faith, the army of unalterable law," who watch from the bookshelves.

In all three of these poems, the New England milieu is examined and rejected. In *Mr. Apollinax*, as already seen, a British lion is favorably contrasted with it. The poems of the next several years were to be marked by further sardonic evaluations, by sometimes bitter or ironic rejection of self and of social customs and institutions, by the side-thrusts of a clearly displaced set of personae attempting to salvage and come to terms with new identities. Even on the far side of the Atlantic, all was not well—as the following poems indicate.

Le Directeur, one of four French poems presumably written in 1916-17, rejects not only the staid periodical *The Spectator* but also its director, smug in his reactionary conservatism. Short lines and repeated rhymes add ironic and laconic overtones to the picture. In *Mélange Adultère de Tout*—a poem modeled (as Grover Smith points out) on Corbière's *Epitaphe pour Tristan-Joachim-Edouard Corbière, Philosophe: Epave, Mort-Né*—both the hollowness of accomplishments and the protagonist himself are cynically commented on.

In *Lune de Miel* the romantic European honeymoon tour outlined in Baedeker's tourist guidebook is shown in the unsatisfactory light of an American couple only slightly aware at best of the glory that is (was?) Europe, but painfully aware of their expenses and the two hundred bedbugs sharing their accommodations at Ravenna. They ignore the nearby glories of the Cathedral of Saint Apollinaire. The *Ode* of Eliot's 1920 volume *Ara Vos Prec* negatively evaluates a perhaps similar honeymoon. (An inferior poem, it has not been allowed inclusion in any later printings of Eliot's poetry.)

The characters of *Dans le restaurant* are the protagonist-customer and a rather unsavory old waiter who hangs over the customer's shoulder and tells him of a deeply impressive seven-year-old experience strongly reminiscent of the first meeting between Dante and Beatrice in the *Vita Nuova*. The customer is outraged to find that his own highest experiences are much like those of the blubbering and repulsive waiter and sends him away. Both this part of the poem and the final stanza on Phlebas the Phoenician (later translated in *The Waste Land*) suggest that certain experiences have universal significance. One should note also, however, the implied criticism of the customer's assumptions of superiority.

In the eight quatrains of *The Hippopotamus* (1917), both rapier and bludgeon are turned against the devitalized institution of The True Church (as opposed to the uncapitalized true church). In contrast, the hippopotamus seems to represent at first the fallible individual human with all his limitations. At the end, it is suggested that perhaps the "True Church" is the hippopotamus, mud-bound, whereas fallible man may ascend to heaven and be blessed by the choiring angels.

Apeneck Sweeney, another wonder of solid flesh destined to figure engagingly if somewhat paradoxically in several other poems within the following years, is similarly weighed against the earthly institution of the church in *Mr. Eliot's Sunday Morning Service*. Like the bees gathering pollen, the earthly church tries to mediate between the individual like Sweeney, sitting in his bath, and the spiritual reality symbolized in the

painting of Christ's baptism by "a painter of the Umbrian school."
It has little success.

Whispers of Immortality, another poem in quatrains, distils
the essence of the appeal for Eliot of such writers as Webster
and Donne, who "found no substitute for sense, to seize and
clutch and penetrate." The poem implies that this thirst for
experience, this "fever of the bone" which could not be allayed
by any "contact possible to flesh," is what enabled these men to
write so impressively. The second half of the poem presents the
protagonist's speculations on Grishkin, who might be a close
relative to Clavdia Chauchat in Thomas Mann's *The Magic
Mountain*. Eliot's description of Grishkin—"Uncorseted, her
friendly bust/Gives promise of pneumatic bliss"—plays ebulliently
on the dual meanings of *pneumatic*. The first is taken from the
Gnostics and from Origen (who was cited in *Mr. Eliot's Sunday
Morning Service*): "PNEUMA . . . the vital soul or the spirit;—
variously interpreted as the animal soul mediating between the
higher spiritual nature and the body, as the breath or life-giving
principle, and as the spirit superior to both soul and body."
The other and more common definition needs no elaboration in
these days of the automobile tire.

Grishkin's temptations are not only to earthly pleasure but
also to a genuine grasp of experience; but the protagonist, more
inclined to philosophy than to exploratory experience, will not
seize and clutch and penetrate because "our lot crawls between
dry ribs/To keep our metaphysics warm."

A "cooking egg" is one no longer fresh enough to eat alone,
and Eliot's poem *A Cooking Egg* equates the protagonist's
marriage with such an egg. Such marital stalemates will be
further explored in the "A Game of Chess" section of *The Waste
Land*; in the present poem its flat qualities are contrasted with
the honor of Sir Philip Sidney, the financial security of Sir
Alfred Mond, the society of Lucretia Borgia, the willingness of
Madame Blavatsky to teach, and the contentment of Piccarda di
Donati. The beginning of Voltaire's *Candide* is suggested in
the lines

> But where is the penny world I bought
> To eat with Pipit behind the screen?

And that world, the visioned world of happy marriage, is gone
like the eagles and the trumpets, "buried beneath some snow-
deep alps." Precious little consolation is found in the even

worse lot of the "Weeping, weeping multitudes/[who] Droop in a hundred A.B.C.'s [chain cafes]."

Venice is the setting of *Burbank with a Baedeker: Bleistein with a Cigar.* The idealist Burbank, the chief character, is a tourist with his Baedeker guidebook that suggests and identifies the glories of Venice—"the great bronze horses over the doors of St. Mark's" and "Tiepolo's great frescoes of Antony and Cleopatra in the Pallazio Labia."[1] Burbank knows his literature and esthetics as well as his Baedeker, but in his attempts to mediate between the ideal and his own "fever of the bone" (*Whispers of Immortality*), he has met Princess Volupine at a small hotel where "They were together, and he fell." The Princess' name suggests both "voluptuous" and "supine," and may remind the post-1922 reader of the Thames-daughter of Richmond origin who appears in section III of *The Waste Land*; at any rate, Burbank's fall is less heroic than that of Adam. Now by the dim, flickering light of "the smoky candle end of time," little glory is apparent from the narrowed perspectives of the fallen Burbank as he watches the "Princess" prepare to entertain her next customer, Sir Ferdinand Klein. This name echoes the various contrasts between the ideal and the immediate throughout the poem. It reminds us that Burbank is no Antony to the Princess' watered-down Cleopatra, no Othello to her mock Desdemona.

Burbank meditates on these contrasts, watches the "lustreless protrusive eye" of Bleistein stare blankly at Canaletto's painting, considers "the proud winged lion on its pillar by the waterfront" and the frescoes. Striving for a non-committal position somewhere between such extremes, he muses on "time's ruins and the seven laws," wondering "Who clipped the lion's wings/ And flea'd his rump and pared his claws?"

Most of the allusions in the poem—and this poem borrows and alludes as heavily as will *The Waste Land* later—are to works related to Venice. A line from the epigraph, "Nothing endures unless divine; all else is smoke," reminds us, if such a jog were needed, that Burbank, as well as Bleistein, lacks the stuff that endurance is made of—or perhaps not; perhaps it is only the experience and vision that created and that appreciate the more-than-beauty of the monuments that endure, not The Stones of Venice themselves.

Except for the Sweeney poems and *Gerontion,* no other new

poems appeared in the 1919 volume *Poems* nor in the 1920 *Ara Vos Prec*.

I *The Sweeney Poems*

Sweeney first appeared briefly and informally in *Mr. Eliot's Sunday Morning Service*: In just two lines, we read, "Sweeney shifts from ham to ham/Stirring the water in his bath." Presumably even this vignette can be assimilated into their theologies by "The masters of the subtle schools/[who] Are controversial, polymath." And the reader, who has been considering the implied three-way comparisons between the rejected representatives of the devitalized earthly church, the worker bees at their business of intermediating between "The staminate and pistilate," and the unoffending feet of Christ in a bas-relief by a painter of the Umbrian school, finds Sweeney's vigor and directness not wholly objectionable; in this attraction lies a clue to the self-criticism of the title. In it lies also evidence that the author does not wholly reject Sweeney, any more than Yeats wholly rejects his Crazy Jane. Usually when Sweeney appears, some degree of criticism against those who consider themselves greatly superior to him hovers in the background behind the sometimes gross figure that he cuts. So Sweeney in this poem takes on a slightly enigmatic character, but even so he contrasts not entirely disadvantageously with the timid esthetes like Prufrock who appear in the early poems.

He is more clearly characterized in *Sweeney Erect*, but the reader is allowed less sympathy with him. This poem is focused on desertions classical and otherwise, the latest and most "otherwise" being the one that Sweeney is about to commit. It is set in the distorted world of Mrs. Turner's "house." Presumably this is another version of the establishment of Mrs. Porter seen in *The Waste Land* and in *Sweeney Agonistes*. Doris appears in both casts, and the epileptic on the bed, whom Sweeney deserts, may well be her friend Dusty.

In this world the classical stature and vitality of Homer's Odysseus, Nausicaa, and Polyphemus are weakly echoed by the "I" of the poem, the ape-like Sweeney, and the epileptic who, for him, represents "the female temperament." Potential social tragedy is almost lost for lack of a proper audience, though the commenting persona suggests by calling them Nausicaa and

Polyphemus that he rejects and will leave these people and this situation. Still "Odysseus" is appearing in this company, even if he *can* transmute Beaumont and Fletcher and quote Emerson's definition of history as "the lengthened shadow of a man" to Sweeney's disadvantage.

Similar contrasts between the classical heroic and the hushed and shrunken scene of Sweeney in a bawdyhouse are found in *Sweeney Among the Nightingales*. Mysterious identities, threats of violence, and whispers of intrigue create an oppressive, foreboding atmosphere. The setting reminds us of the "Circe" chapter of James Joyce's *Ulysses;* in fact, quite a few details of Leopold Bloom's book seem relevant to Sweeney in his various poems, which were written at a time when Pound and Eliot were championing Joyce and specifically *Ulysses* in the desperate struggle for publication in the face of moral(?) indignation among almost all English-language publishers, and through Pound's efforts *Ulysses* was being serialized in *The Little Review*.

In *Sweeney Among the Nightingales* the reader is again allowed an ambivalent sympathy with Sweeney; in *Mr. Eliot's Sunday Morning Service* Sweeney compared favorably to "enervate Origen" for reasons involved in the present poem's setting, and now he compares favorably to Rachel of the murderous paws and to the other indistinct, threatening characters, four or possibly five of them, who lurk on the edges of our field of clear vision.[2] The paralleling of Agamemnon adds tragic overtones relevant not just to Sweeney but to the whole moral ambience of the poem. Sweeney does take on added significance in that new light, because we see that he represents a general moral axiom: Deal in psychic acts like these, associate with those who do, frequent this sort of setting, and you too, lecteur, will suffer the risk of violent and bloody passions. The resultant purgation of pity and fear is further pursued in Eliot's unfinished first venture into overt drama (or rather Aristophanic melodrama), the projected play *Wanna Go Home, Baby?*, of which only the two fragments entitled *Sweeney Agonistes* were written.

Matthiessen sums up Sweeney's significance when he says that "the double feeling of [Eliot's] repulsion from vulgarity, and yet his shy attraction to the coarse earthiness of common life have found their complete symbol in Sweeney."[3]

II Gerontion

We may infer from its initial position in the 1920 volume *Ara Vos Prec* that *Gerontion* was the poem then most esteemed by the author of the new works included there—and perhaps the most recent. Eliot's letters to Pound show that later, in 1922, he considered using it as a prelude to *The Waste Land,* and its relevance to the dryness of that later, more widely analyzed poem has been often suggested. Nevertheless, *Gerontion* remains the least understood, I believe, of Eliot's major poems— and that is not because of any great or insuperable difficulty. What has been overlooked is the poem's simplicity. Though it is true that history is one of the poem's topics and the efficacy of Christianity another, *Gerontion* is an intensely personal poem, and the clarity and unity of its structure are obscured by failing sufficiently to relate those broader themes to the immediate experience of the persona who is its protagonist. The title means "little old man."

In form, the poem approximates a letter, as is suggested by the lines from Fitzgerald's letters on which the beginning of *Gerontion* is based and by the documents of Sigismundo Malatesta (pondered on in Ezra Pound's *Malatesta Cantos*), who fought "knee deep in the salt marsh." The letter is addressed to a "you" who is asked to think of various things and to whom Gerontion says "I would meet you upon this honestly" and further explains why "I that was near your heart was removed therefrom." Gerontion meditates on and assesses his past and present quite intimately, and might be suspected of wanting to make an exhibition of himself. But he assures the addressee that "I have not made this show purposelessly/And it is not by any concitation [stirring up or excitation]/Of the backward devils" (presumably as in Conrad's *Heart of Darkness*). He meditates on his own history, the most important element of which is the quest of a proper love on a sexual-religious plane.

In the spring of his life, "the juvescence of the year," sprang Christ the Tiger. The Christian symbols for the Primal Love toward which Gerontion's *amor* might properly have been directed were not in his youth clearly perceived nor experienced. His token participation in the devitalized and misunderstood sacraments of his "Christian" culture was shared with equally or more mis-oriented associates, and so he rejected both the divinity behind the rituals and the divinity in men which might have left him with some ghosts, holy or otherwise. Now much time has passed, as have many of the "supple confusions" of history which make of experiences often the opposite of our intentions and expectations, leaving us sadder but wiser.

In the light of such knowledge comes a new Spring. Such a sign of Primal Love as Christ can be recognized, and the lesser loves, the attachments to the appetites, are surrendered—devoured, perhaps, in fashion similar to the devouring of the leopards in the later poem *Ash-Wednesday*. Gerontion, then, in his draughty house, deliberates on the nature of his loves, higher and lower; and he explains to the person addressed the significance of their altered relationship.

In the first stanza he speaks of himself as "an old man in a dry month,/Being read to by a boy" (a near-quote from Fitzgerald's letters). He is waiting for the rain that is so urgently desired in *The Waste Land*. He disowns any impressive history, having neither been "at the hot gates/Nor fought in the warm rain," nor has he "knee deep in the salt marsh, heaving a cutlass,/Bitten by flies, fought." These allusions are to the history of Sigismundo, as reflected in Pound's cantos. The decayed house metaphor suggests the twelfth chapter of Ecclesiastes (a passage cited by Eliot in his notes to *The Waste Land*), in which a house is similarly used to represent the body and the senses.

In yet another sense, Gerontion's house is post-World War I Western culture, somewhat "gone in the teeth." And the lines "And the jew squats on the window sill, the owner,/Spawned in some estaminet of Antwerp,/Blistered in Brussels, patched and peeled in London" seem to suggest three things: first, perhaps, on the literal level, the owner of the actual house that Gerontion rents in London; second, Christ (or God), the owner of the body for which "house" is a metaphor and of the soul that inhabits it, however unresponsive to his claims Gerontion may at times have been; and third, the Jewish international bankers who, Eliot evidently believed, participated heavily in the collapse of civilized Europe through World War I. There is also, of course, the suggestion of the Judeo-Christian culture from which most of our religions and much of our Western culture derive. And I take it that all of these are demonstrably important and intertwined in this poem. James Joyce's treatment of Leopold Bloom in the "Cyclops" chapter of *Ulysses* combines and emphasizes such themes and was almost certainly familiar to Eliot at the time of writing *Gerontion.*

Gerontion's years seem qualified in the epigraph ("Thou hast nor youth nor age . . ."), and perhaps further by the second line, "Being read to by a boy. . . ." I would suggest that, like the house metaphor, in which the windows are the eyes, aspects of Gerontion himself are represented by the boy and by the woman who keeps the kitchen; she might in Jungian terms represent the anima, or in the terms of *The Cocktail Party,* the "tougher self," which cannot be suppressed without causing trouble. Similarly, Gerontion's goat which coughs at night and field overhead seem to be parts of himself suggesting the libido and the field of awareness behind conscious daytime thought. In lines 17-20, the theme of Christ is introduced in the "Word" or *"Logos"* passage that Eliot has used frequently (as, for example, in *Mr. Eliot's Sunday Morning Service, Ash-Wednesday,* and elsewhere); and we are reminded of the beginning of Gerontion's life, as of the creation and, especially in this context, the birth of Christ. Eliot was consciously referring to a sermon of Lancelot Andrewes which speaks of "verbum infans," the word within a word, unable to speak a word—a passage cited by Eliot in his essay "For Lancelot Andrewes."

In the line " 'We would see a sign,' " we are reminded of Matthew 16 and John 6, in which Christ is asked for a sign that he is the son of God. In Matthew 16:4, he replies "A wicked and adulterous generation seeketh after a sign; and there shall no sign be given unto it, but the sign of the prophet Jonas." In John, Christ replies that he is the sign. And in *Gerontion* again Christ is the sign, "The word within a word, unable to speak a word." And many other signs, Gerontion implies, are all about us; but wonders are desired, not signs. Yet Christ *is* a wonder, though rejected and unrecognized. So both in the individual life of Gerontion and in the life of Western culture, past and present, the sign is unrecognized and the nativity is followed by depraved May, the season of crucifixion; and the sacraments are perverted and parodied.

In Gerontion's experience the nearest things to the mysterious communion that could result from the proper acceptance of the divine in man, symbolized in Christianity and in all major religions by incarnation, is the overtures made "by Mr. Silvero, with caressing hands . . ./By Hakagawa, bowing among the Titians" (works of a painter who *did* understand); by Madame de Tornquist, who shifted the candles, having the scene arrange itself, as in *Portrait of a Lady*; and by Fraulein von Kulp, who turned and looked invitingly as she was about to enter her room.

The depraved May imagery is derived from the *Education of Henry Adams* passage in which Adams depicts the rank luxuriousness and the depravity of the Washington spring and contrasts it with the stringent moral tone of New England. The overtones of perverted power, justice, and vigor and of debased potentialities are echoes in the hollow corridors of Gerontion's memory. So for those who in the youth of the individual life or of the culture reject the incarnation—the sign of the vital principle, the first mover, the higher love—the most potent rituals can only be parodied. But Gerontion either did not accept or has transcended those invitations: he has no ghosts, and only vacant shuttles weave the wind in his draughty house. His sexual-religious aspirations were unfulfilled or the sexual were replaced by religious ones; through these rejections he has arrived at his present state.

The next section of *Gerontion*—perhaps justly the most widely admired lines in the poem—discusses the ways in which "history" produces dry brains like Gerontion's: she deceives by whispering ambitions and vanities; she "Gives too late/What's not believed in" or "too soon/Into weak hands. . . ." This section of the poem asks the addressee to think about these things and finally to think that "Neither fear nor courage saves us. Unnatural vices/ Are fathered by our heroism. Virtues/Are forced upon us by our impudent crimes." But all has not been in vain, and all hope has not been lost, for the tiger springs in the new year, and "Us he devours."

Having seen the emptiness of all the substitute solutions, Gerontion has found a meaning in his life. He assures the person addressed that neither his life nor his poem ("this show") has been made purposelessly, nor "by any concitation/Of the backward devils." His purpose in his poem is to help the reader to understand not just his plight and actions, his "desertion," but also the possibilities open to one who sees the falseness of the *parodied* vitality, to one who can recognize and accept the signs as wonders without first wasting most of a lifetime tramping empty corridors. He is reconciled now to his place in the universal cycles, approaching the end of life and the dissolution of death.

Like millions of others before him, like De Bailhache, Fresca, and Mrs. Cammel, he will be "whirled/Beyond the circuit of the shuddering Bear/In fractured atoms," but this is the universal fate, the proper pattern, and is common both to those who fight at the warm gates ("Gull against the wind, in the windy straits") and to "an old man driven by the Trades/To a sleepy corner"; and what is necessary now is to make the most of what remains. So the profit of what is past is protracted and perhaps shared through "These with a thousand small deliberations." Awareness of all this will not alter the universe: the spider and the weevil will continue their spinning and destruction. But the calm acceptance will be better than the vain pursuit of illusions, and Gerontion has surrendered his romanticism, seeing now the divinity in common humanity. Like Plato or Aristotle, he waits for the death wind without fear and loathing: in Christian terms, he looks forward to a higher life after death, which he will regard as liberation from the dry brain and the decayed house—to the life of the undistracted spirit rather than of the small deliberations.

This interpretation, of course, disagrees with the usual dating of the turn to Christianity in Eliot's poetry; and it also foreshadows a reading of *The Waste Land* in much less negative terms than are usually applied to it.

CHAPTER 4

Why Then Ile Fit You

FEW CRITICS SEEM to have followed up Eliot's suggestion that *Gerontion* is the best prelude to *The Waste Land*, and those who have done so have usually misread both poems as expressing only aridity, waste, and despair. When *The Waste Land* appeared in 1922, it was greeted by critical acclaim on the one hand and by expressions of outrage on the other. Some charged that Eliot was perpetrating a great hoax on the literary world. Of the general favorable reactions, Eliot remarked in 1931, "I dislike the word 'generation,' which has been a talisman for the last ten years; when I wrote a poem called *The Waste Land* some of the more approving critics said that I had expressed the 'disillusionment of a generation,' which is nonsense. I may have expressed for them their own illusion of being disillusioned, but that did not form part of my intention."[1]

Though much of the technique of the poem had been seen in embryo as early as *Prufrock* and in more developed and involved form in *Burbank with a Baedeker, Mr. Eliot's Sunday Morning Service,* and *Sweeney Among the Nightingales,* the reader could in each of those poems follow a developing narrative of a sort. *The Waste Land,* however, like *Gerontion,* is a meditation by a speaker whose nature must be intuited from the materials, tone, and perspectives of the poem. The conscious links—the overt connections between the various materials making up the poem—are omitted and must be supplied by the reader via the inferences he can draw, which gradually make him aware of the precise center from which the poem is spoken. Like *Gerontion, The Waste Land* is intensely personal, and the basis of its technique and progression lies in a highly individualized consciousness.

The necessity to transcend one's self is a basic theme of the poem. Further, social responsibility is at the very core of the mythic and traditional elements combined in it. Eliot's social consciousness is widely documented in such essays as *The Idea of a Christian Society* and in a number of his critical writings such as the early "Tradition and the Individual Talent." That the unifying ground of the poem in the mind of the speaker (the term "persona" seems less appropriate for this poem than for poems previously discussed because of the lack of posing—this poem is a meditation rather than an "observation") has gone unnoticed by many readers is due to the poem's startlingly original form and techniques. These divergences from earlier usage are in no sense arbitrary and pointless, but highly functional; they are matters of scale and degree, not of kind.

D. H. Lawrence spoke of the necessity of writing poetry "without a shadow of a lie, or a shadow of deflection anywhere." "Everything can go," he continued, "but this stark, bare, rocky directness of statement, this alone makes poetry, to-day."[2] In 1933, Eliot remarked on Lawrence's statement,

> This speaks to me of that at which I have long aimed, in writing poetry; to write poetry which should be essentially poetry, with nothing [un]poetic about it, poetry standing naked in its bare bones, or poetry so transparent that we should not see the poetry, but that which we are meant to see through the poetry, poetry so transparent that in reading it we are intent on what the poem *points at*, and not on the poetry, this seems to me the thing to try for. To get *beyond poetry*, as Beethoven, in his later works, strove to get *beyond music*. We never succeed, perhaps . . .[3]

But certainly Eliot came very near to succeeding in *The Waste Land*: it is only by seeing through to what the poem points at that it can be read at all *as poetry*.

Gerontion, as we have seen him above, would make a not-at-all-inappropriate speaker for this poem: He has known the themes of *The Waste Land*, and has hinted at the cultural and esthetic awarenesses basic to the method of the poem. The Elizabethan dramatists who strongly influenced the verse-forms in *Gerontion* will appear in this poem in both the content and perspectives of the verse. For this poem, it is helpful—but not indispensable—to be familiar with Wagnerian opera; the vegetative rites discussed in Sir James Frazer's *The Golden Bough*; the related Grail legends and the Tarot pack of cards discussed in Jessie L. Weston's *From Ritual to Romance*; Christian ritual and tradition including the works of Dante and St. Augustine and the liturgy of the Anglican church; a good bit of Greek, Latin, French, and English literature (with a little German thrown in); and some Buddhist and Hindu religious classics.

The Waste Land is a consciously stylized utterance directed to twentieth-century readers. At times the protagonist directly addresses them; at other times he recalls from his past history, much as Gerontion did, elements which have had moral or spiritual significance for him, and which focus on or are analogous to the components and the course of his own psychic history. His memories, comments, and meditations are presented to the reader with varying degrees of directness; and these shifting modes of address seem to me to reproduce accurately the varieties of awareness normal to human experience. Quite a number of "personages" are referred to in the poem or are used as vehicles for the speaker's expression, each of them having close and important connections with the struggle for psychic fulfillment or maturity.

The most important of these are the "Fisher King" of the Grail legends; "The Hanged Man" of the Tarot pack of cards; the drowned Phoenician sailor Phlebas; Ferdinand, Prince of Naples, from Shakespeare's *The Tempest*; Christ; Tristan; Parsifal; St. Augustine; certain biblical prophets; Tiresias, the blind Theban seer of Homer's *Odyssey*, Euripides' *Bacchae* and *Phoenissae*, and Sophocles' Theban plays; and the three Thames-daughters patterned after the Rhine-daughters of Wagner's *Ring of the Nibelungs* tetralogy. Though the speaker of the poem identifies in varying degrees with each of these personages, he still seems always present as the filtering and uttering consciousness; the framework which gives each his proper place in the poem is not inherent in any one of them, though it may have analogs in each one's history.

I *The Symbols*

When the poem was first printed in book form two months after its initial publication in the *Criterion* of October, 1922, the printer needed additional copy to fill a signature; since Eliot had no other poems ready at that time, he submitted the explanatory notes on *The Waste Land* which now fill about five pages in the *Complete Poems and Plays, 1909-1950*. The notes have been the focus of much critical effort and comment, and Eliot has since remarked that he regrets having appended them. One valuable function of the notes, nevertheless, has been to indicate some of the works that most importantly influenced the writing of the poem—among others (as we mentioned) Frazer's *The Golden Bough* and Weston's *From Ritual to Romance,* books relevant to much of the basic symbolism used. In the vegetative rites discussed in both, the figure of the Year-god was thrown into the waters of the Nile (or some other body of water) and later "fished out" (resurrected), symbolizing the rebirth of the life principle in the spring. This ritual also came to be associated with the religious initiation patterns to which primitive people seem to give much more open recognition than do modern civilized societies. The Grail legends, according to Miss Weston, are derived from those vegetative rites, and it is the Fisher King on whom the health and fertility of the land and people are dependent in these legends. The Fisher King is sick, having been maimed (usually a sexual wound); and, because he is sick, his lands are waste and barren, just as in *Oedipus Rex* (as Tiresias knew) the plague upon Thebes was due to the crimes of Oedipus against the procreative cycles. Only when the Fisher King is healed through the appearing of a pure fool who asks the proper questions can the land again become fertile.

The relevance of this to the Christian scheme is discussed by Miss Weston; it is summarized as follows by G. S. Fraser: "The Christian interpretation of this traditional myth is the highest one: the sacrificed king is Christ, as God Incarnate, and the barren land which has to be reclaimed to fertility is the human heart, full of selfishness and lust, choked with the tares of sin."[4] The inevitability of the "fish" and "fisher" religious symbolism is seen by reflecting on the high degree to which the early peoples were dependent on rivers and seas, the fecundity and vitality of fishes, and the mysterious "grace" which brings the fish to the fisherman. Thus Buddha, for one example, was represented as sitting on the bank of the ocean of Samsara, casting for the fish of Truth to draw it to the light of salvation;[5] and Christ, for another, offered to make his disciples "fishers of men."

Another important set of symbols related to the Grail legends and to the vegetative rites is seen in the Tarot cards, which are used in Section I of *The Waste Land* by Madame Sosostris, the fortune-teller, to read the fortune of the speaker. These cards, of uncertain origin, have been used for centuries for fortune-telling in general, and more specifically for predicting the rise and fall of the waters which brought fertility to the land.[6] Of the Madame Sosostris section of *The Waste Land,* F. R. Leavis has said, ". . . it at once intimates the scope of the

poem, the mode of its contemplation of life. It informs us as
to the nature of the characters: we know that they are such as
could not have relations with one another in any narrative
scheme, and could not be brought together on any stage, no
matter what liberties were taken with the Unities. . . ."[7]

Eliot has somewhat altered the Tarot deck to fit his own
purposes, and the ways in which he has done so are indicative
of the synthetic "mythic method" underlying the whole poem.
His use of the Tarot pack was very likely influenced by his
close friend Charles Williams, whose novel *The Greater Trumps*[8]
is built around Tarot symbols. In his introduction to that novel,
William Lindsay Gresham writes of "the wise old man, and two
dominant symbols—water, signifying the unconscious itself, and
the mandala-wheel of integration, divided into quadrants by the
cross, the mighty sign of four." Each of these is quite relevant
to Eliot's writings, including *The Waste Land*, as are a number
of Mr. Gresham's comments on the greater trumps, especially
those on the Lovers, Fortitude, the Hanged Man, Death, the
Devil, and the Moon.

Many critics have written of the antitheses, the antinomies,
and the contrasts in *The Waste Land*. These exist in abundance
and are not just accidents of inclusion; they comprise a basic and
indispensable aspect of the poem's technique, progression, and
meaning. Many such polarities could be identified in the
poem: universal-personal, male-female, conscious-unconscious,
hope-fear, and others. But the technique of contradiction goes
deeper than this in the poem's structure. Many of its symbols
are involved in what I should like to call "parallelodoxes." Many
of its symbols, that is, simultaneously develop in antithetical
directions. The symbol of water, for instance, is already present
ambiguously in line nine of the first section: The shower of
rain that comes over the Starnbergersee both heralds the summer
and makes the speaker run for shelter.

The absence of water and the thirst for it enter in line 24, "the
dry stone [gives] no sound of water"; in line 42, *"Oed und leer
das Meer"* ("Wide and empty the sea"), water is both a negative
and a positive symbol: it may carry Isolde and her healing arts
to the dying Tristan, but as yet it is waste and barren. The fear
of death by water is first made explicit by Madame Sosostris.
Both sides of this ambiguous symbol are inconspicuously present
in the game of chess: "The hot water at ten./And if it rains, a
closed car at four"; and again the negative side is seen through

the allusion to Ophelia, who drowned herself: "Good night, ladies, good night, sweet ladies, good night, good night."

In Section III, "The Fire Sermon," the river has both positive and negative connotations, suggesting both purity and pollution, both innocence and immorality. Mrs. Porter's soda water is contrasted with the ceremonial water of the Grail chapel in Verlaine's *Parsifal*. This parallel but antithetical development is amplified in great detail throughout the poem. Death by water, which in Section I was to be feared, has become by Section IV ambiguous—suggesting both the dissolution of physical death and the promise of resurrection in the Year-god ceremonies, Christian baptism, the Easter pageant, and the other chief symbolic patterns used.

The symbol of Philomel provides another such "parallelodox": in its first appearance, again, we see both positive and negative connotations:

> Above the antique mantel was displayed
> As though a window gave upon the sylvan scene
> The change of Philomel, by the barbarous king
> So rudely forced; yet there the nightingale
> Filled all the desert with inviolable voice
> And still she cried and still the world pursues,
> "Jug Jug" to dirty ears.

In context this passage suggests not only the beauty of a remote and picturesque artifact but also the cruel violation suffered by Philomel; her song, the "inviolable voice" ("twit twit") still sounds like "jug jug" to dirty ears. She next appears in Section III, "The Fire Sermon," after the contradictory references to Mrs. Porter and *"ces voix d'enfants, chantant dans la coupole"* ("those voices of children, singing in the choir-loft"): "Twit twit twit/ Jug jug jug jug jug jug/So rudely forc'd/Tereu." The irony of the reference to Verlaine's Grail ceremony in this context carries over into the song of the nightingale, at first positive, then negative. The next line, "So rudely forc'd," refers not only to Philomel but also to the use of Grail imagery in the "Sweeney and Mrs. Porter" context. The closing word of this four-line passage, "Tereu," suggests Tereus's act of violation, the fact that it is to be rued, and the sound of the bird's singing; for "twit twit," "jug jug," and "Tereu" were the three common representations of the nightingale's song in Elizabethan literature, where its moral meanings were emphasized as they are here.

Though Philomel does not appear again directly in *The Waste Land*, she is suggested in the other bird songs used and referred to at two levels of indirectness in the *"Quando fiam uti chelidon"* fragment ("When will I be like the swallow?") of the closing passage for the reader who is familiar with its context in the anonymous Latin work *Pervigilium Veneris*. As in the case of the water symbol, which by the end of the poem suggested the whole principle which Jung calls the "anima," the associations of the Philomel symbol have been expanded by the entire development of the poem: By the end she has come to suggest in all their varieties both violation through lust and purification through transformation. Fire is similarly used and developed as the symbol of both the destroying lust which must be transcended and the purgatorial flames which purify.

Such "parallelodoxes" are inevitable concomitants of the associative method by which the poem develops in the mind of the speaker. Its associational basis is not in ideas or images, but in total states of a complex and individual consciousness that is always aware of multiple implications. This sort of progression is implicit in the poem's entire structure, but it is easy to miss, since its recognition arises in the reader's empathic identification—"You! hypocrite lecteur!—mon semblable,—mon frère!" The requirement of this identification necessarily limits the readership of the poem, but it also allows degrees of compression and of subtle complexity probably impossible to achieve by any other structural technique. The poem is essentially dramatic, and its appreciation depends on what Francis Fergusson calls "the histrionic sensibility." But both the stage and the cast of the poem exist in the mind of the speaker. It is true that often we need to recognize the personages through whom he speaks, but always we need to recognize as well the tone and emphasis of his voice speaking through them.

II Dantean Scheme and Intent

Eliot wrote in 1935 that he wanted literature to be unconsciously rather than deliberately and defiantly Christian. This statement, of course, refers to technique as well as to content. In the same essay is expressed the view that reading does affect our moral and religious existence, and that the greatness of literature is not determined solely by literary standards: the poet's job is to present to his readers true worldly wisdom, which will lead up to other-worldly wisdom, and will be completed and fulfilled by it.[9]

As we emphasized in Chapter 2, Dante exerted a very strong influence on Eliot's use of the Christian tradition, and especially on his use of its rituals in *The Waste Land*: the crucifixion and resurrection; baptism; and the burial ritual and liturgy, from which the first section of the poem takes its title. (The Mass is dramatically embodied in the Earthly Paradise and Paradise sections of Dante's *Divine Comedy*. Eliot followed that lead in writing *The Rock, Murder in the Cathedral*, and especially *Ash-Wednesday*.)

The Dantean scheme and intent are central to the unity and to the proper interpretation of *The Waste Land*. The most immediately obvious borrowings from the *Divine Comedy* are seen in the "crowd flowing over London Bridge" passage of Section I and in the *"Poi s'ascose nel foco che gli affina"* quotation at the end of the poem. Dante's influence, however, permeates the whole poem, as a number of critics who compare it to Dante's *Inferno* have noted. Philo M. Buck, in his *Directions in Contemporary Literature*, wrote of the "irrelevant waste and despair that knows not its emptiness" seen in *The Waste Land*, and he further pointed out that the purpose of Dante's *Inferno* is to make unregenerate humanity see, "with no veil to obscure, the ugliness of sin. Evil must be stripped of all of its false allure and stand before the poet naked, grotesque, and un-ashamed, not that he may recoil at its horror and stand in judgement . . . but that he may suffer in mind and body the moral illness that is necessary before the discipline of Purgatory can be begun."[10]

This confrontation is precisely what the speaker of *The Waste Land* tries to accomplish for the wastelanders. We see in the poem not the expression of such emptiness, but rather its description. That is, the attitudes depicted are not those of the speaker, but rather states that he has recognized and transcended (as Mr. Buck goes on to point out).

Thus the speaker, by recognizing its anatomy and significance, has passed out of hell, where no psychic postures except those observed are conceivable; and he has made the difficult transition into purgation of his damning tendencies—has exercised "the good of the intellect." He is aware of the antithetical poles of the poem's symbols, aware now of the depths of its negative implications but also the height of its positive dimensions. He is aware both of "the prison" (involvement with the profitless aspects of the immediate) and of "the key." And thanks to the collocation in his mind of Buddha's "Fire Sermon," Shakespeare's *The Tempest,* the three commands of the Hindu thunder myth, Christ's resurrection, St. Augustine's reversal, the Fisher King's restoration, and the other echoes in the poem, he is aware of the means needed to complete the transformation in his psychic focus to the high felicity of a properly ordered love. Hell, then, is represented in *The Waste Land* only through images. His contemporaries and readers, to whom the speaker addresses himself, are, like him, still living; and they have yet the possibility of putting the intellect to its good and proper use.

Eliot, like Dante, tries to stimulate his reader to do so by showing first—using language to communicate to the reader's bones and muscles—the feel of inferno, and then by introducing guides from literature and tradition, both classical and contemporary, who help one understand what he has seen and felt. And just as Dante has philosophical passages in which Virgil, Statius, Marco Lombardo, Beatrice, and others explain to Dante what he has already experienced so that he will understand it, will "use the good of the intellect," Eliot occasionally in the earlier poems and much more frequently in *Ash-Wednesday* and in the *Four Quartets* has written philosophical poetry aimed at the understanding of the reader as well as at his senses—the senses whose appeal the reader must transcend in order to escape inferno. *The Waste Land,* however, omits all such explicit statements.

The speaker sees his contemporaries largely in those attitudes of soul symbolized in Dante's *Inferno* either by the trimmers—who "lived without blame, and without praise" and who are admitted neither to heaven nor the depths of hell (Dante's description of them is echoed in the lines "A crowd flowed over London Bridge, so many,/I had not thought death had undone so many")—or by the shades in Limbo who lived and died before Christianity and thus without baptism. Though they were virtuous, these latter shades occupy the first circle of Dante's hell (their description is echoed in Eliot's lines "Sighs, short and infrequent, were exhaled,/And each man fixed his eyes before his feet"). But only if Eliot's Londoners are caught by death and frozen in such attitudes of the soul will they partake of hell.

The meeting with Stetson (the reader) echoes the many

passages in which Dante converses with the shades he and Virgil encounter in hell, and the Arnaut Daniel fragment at the end of the poem focuses the relevance to *The Waste Land* of the Dantean scheme. As with more borrowings in this poem than in any other, Eliot demands of his reader for full understanding a familiarity with the broad context of his borrowed line; for he hopes to send his readers on a tour through the works of literature most relevant to the paramount problems of the wastelanders.

Dante the Pilgrim meets Arnaut Daniel in the seventh and last cornice of purgatory, where the lustful are purged. As he previously ascended the stairway to this cornice with his guides, the pagan Virgil and the Christian Statius, the latter has expounded to Dante the doctrine of the development of the soul which further clarifies Marco Lombardo's discourse (already examined above in connection with *Animula*). Statius has linked the soul's history closely to divine love and to the reproductive processes with their sexual basis. Through this discourse, Dante has been brought to understand the mode of existence of the shades populating Dante's hell, purgatory, and heaven.

Similarly, Eliot's reader, in order to understand the workings of *The Waste Land's* imagery and structure, must become aware that the immediate scene, the "unreal city" of London, and the bodies of himself and his contemporaries are much less important than *their* souls.

Virgil's explanation of purgatory emphasizes the fact that Dante (like Eliot's readers) is still alive, and that full repentance before death can bring one to such an advanced stage of purgation as this—to the level of those in purgatory nearest their goal. For Arnaut is encountered shortly before the entrance to the Earthly Paradise at the top of Mount Purgatory. Dante has been allowed to experience these things before death, he says, through the grace of "a Lady above"—through unearned good fortune.

The shades in Cornice VII of the *Purgatorio* are divided into two groups: those who suffer for homosexual lust and those who, though their lusts were heterosexual, "followed them like brute beasts." (Both groups have also been included in *The Waste Land*.) This last conversation with a suffering shade in purgatory indicates approximately the limits beyond which, in Dante's scheme, the unChristian knowledge of Virgil cannot progress. It takes place on the narrow path where those who pass on between the flames and the cliff must go single file, alone; the nature of the progress beyond that point excludes help from outside; and it also requires the withdrawing of attachment to others or of love improperly directed toward them. And it is out of the searing flames that Arnaut addresses Dante.

This necessity of renouncing lust is also the message of Buddha's "Fire Sermon," which like the present passage is couched in fire imagery—though there the fire has only negative connotations; here it symbolizes both the burning flames of lust and the purging flames of proper love. Yet, though one must go alone to be plucked out of the first burning (lust) by the second (love), the plucking enables him to give, sympathize, and control, just as, when the two bands of shades pass in Dante's Cornice VII, each of them quickly kisses one of those in the other group and hurries on. Of this sympathy, this properly directed love, their lust formerly made them incapable.

"What Tiresias sees," "the substance of the poem" according to Eliot's often-misinterpreted note, is therefore the necessity of pure concern for one's fellow-humans without the sins of lust that violate the proper natural order and make individuals incapable of genuine love. Like Dante's Virgil, though, Tiresias in *The Waste Land* lacks the Christian dimension; and he is able to point one only so far as the earthly felicity represented in Dante's scheme by the Earthly Paradise at the top of Mount Purgatory.

When *The Waste Land* appeared in 1922, Eliot already had given frequent hints of his preoccupation with Arnaut's speech, a passage earlier emphasized in Ezra Pound's *The Spirit of Romance*; and in 1920 he had given the title *Ara Vos Prec* to a collection of his poems containing chiefly the observations of Dantean watchers of the fruits of improperly ordered love. He was later to use "*Sovegna vos*" in Part IV of *Ash-Wednesday*, and in his 1929 *Dante* book he quoted the speech both in Provençal and in English translation. Because a number of the Provençal phrases are scattered through Eliot's works, it bears repeating here:

> "Ieu sui Arnaut, que plor e vau cantan;
>   consiros vei la passada folor,
>   e vei jausen lo jorn, qu' esper, denan.
> Ara vos prec, per aquella valor
>   que vos guida al som de l'escalina,
>   sovegna vos a temps de ma dolor."
> POI S' ASCOSE NEL FOCO CHE GLI AFFINA.

("I am Arnold, who weeps and goes singing. I see in thought
all the past folly. And I see with joy the day for which I hope,
before me. And so I pray you, by that Virtue which leads you to
the topmost of the stair—be mindful in due time of my pain."
Then dived he back into that fire which refines them.)[11]

As Arnaut and his fellow shades speak to Dante, they take
great care not to step outside the painful flames which are
purging them. It is crucial to note that their suffering is entirely
voluntary. And this is not just a point of Dante's fiction: It is
Thomistic doctrine. But more importantly, it is a psychological
necessity known to the medical doctor as well as to the
psychologist: the patient must will his own recovery—the bit can
never be removed from the horse's mouth safely until he *wants*
to go in the right direction. What is involved in Dante's
purgatory is not mere punishment, but the willing acceptance
of the effects of misguided, defective, or excessive love which
will make the sufferer aware of the improper nature of his past
acts and will alter or erase his tendencies toward such acts.
Thus at the top of Mount Purgatory he has achieved the regained innocence—not of ignorance but of understanding. And
hence he recognizes the instant when his purgation in any one
cornice of purgatory is complete, and nothing holds him back
to suffer further if his own improper focus does not.

Such also is the nature of escape from Eliot's waste land;
and, like Arnaut Daniel, Eliot's speaker has spoken out of the
cleansing purgatorial fire only long enough to make clear to his
hearers the nature of the place in which he has been met, of the
ravages of lust in its most inclusive sense (the anatomy of hell),
and of the process necessary to its transcendence—"Then dived
he back into the fire that refines them." As Roy Battenhouse
says, Eliot has in his poetry made a vocation of diving back into
the fire.

III *Shape and Development of the Poem*

The over-all shape of the poem is an analogous structure
having parallels in the Year-god ceremonies; the maiming and
eventual healing of the Fisher King; the burial and resurrection
of Christ and of the Christian in baptism; the supposed drowning
of Ferdinand's father, King Alonso, in Shakespeare's *Tempest*,
which eventuates in a real psychic resurrection for him; Dante's
descent into hell, which eventually leads up through purgatory

to the earthly paradise as a prelude to his ascent to paradise; the stealing of the Rhine-gold treasure in Wagner's *Ring of the Nibelungs* tetralogy, eventually returned to its rightful place; and the liberation from lust of Arnaut Daniel's purgation by fire, of Buddha's "Fire Sermon," and of the "Thunder Sermon" from which Eliot takes the three commands Give, Sympathize, and Control. Each of these involves a death-and-resurrection sequence; each of them, be it noted, implies an awareness of positive potentialities growing out of the initial waste and barren condition. So that, rather than merely depicting the disillusionment of a generation and the aridity of twentieth-century culture, *The Waste Land* shows the anatomy of these things, and then it says, "That is not it, at all; here are desirable alternatives, proper eventualities for the individual who may be enmeshed in the toils of those snares."

The development of the poem is something as follows: At the beginning, the protagonist is aware of all these positive potentialities and is striving to fulfill them. He has buried his "Old Man" as Saint Paul advises; he has buried his dead, just as Stetson in Section I has buried the corpse of his involvement in the life of the senses, and he hopes for it to sprout. As will be shown again in *Ash-Wednesday*, the grace of rebirth is not achieved passively and easily; the threshold of assent must be guarded against the recurring desires, against the echoes of the earlier involvement in the life of the lower loves. The speaker recalls from his own past and from his reading of Dante, the Bible, Baudelaire, the Grail legends, a modern novel, a painting that he has seen, Wagner's operas, and other sources that the life of attachment to the senses had to die out before a psychic rebirth was possible; and he recalls also the incidents that symbolize the burial of that dead life.

At the end of Section I, in the "Unreal City" passage, he focuses all of these suggestions on his time and place in London; and he takes pains to see that the reader shall also identify himself with these patterns by stopping him and crying to him, "Stetson!/. . . That corpse you planted last year in your garden,/ Has it begun to sprout?" Stetson, whom the protagonist recognizes, is someone he has known—someone who, like him, buried last year in his garden the corpse of his Old Man (dead through lust) that out of it might sprout a proper love. But the dog of self-involvement and pride, of the libidinous appetites (as in *Marina* and chorus VI of *The Rock*), or of the lust symbolized by Sirius, the Dog Star, in *Sweeney Among the Nightingales* and in the vegetative myths of Frazer's *The Golden Bough,* may dig it up; or the unpredictable accidents or untimely death ("the sudden frost") may disturb its bed. Then lest the reader should fail to understand that it is he who is being addressed, that he is Stetson, the section ends with a direct address quoted from Baudelaire's preface to *Les Fleurs du Mal,* "You! hypocrite reader!—my double,—my brother!"

Section II, "A Game of Chess," depicts the stunting effects of improperly directed love or of lust mistaken for love. In this section we see the pawns moving about in two games that end not in checkmate but in stalemate. The first is set in the boudoir of a lady of means surrounded by symbols and artifacts of the vitality of our cultural heritage. In this setting, however, their vitality has been lost; they are rather "withered stumps of time," symbols no longer valid or not valid for such people and such circumstances. These are the "heap of broken images" that have lost their meaning; the settings of these two seductions and all the others in the poem comprise the stony rubble out of which it is to be hoped that the roots being stirred by spring rain may send forth branches.

This first boudoir scene suggests Joyce's play *The Exiles,* Conrad's story "The Return," Middleton's *Women Beware Women,* and Webster's *The Devil's Law Case,* among other sources. It is paralleled to the ravishing of Philomel by Tereus in Greek legend. The second scene, narrated by an unidentified lower-class lady in a pub at closing time, is overheard by the protagonist. Her life and those lives of which she talks have been consumed by improper loves.

Section III, "The Fire Sermon," takes its title from Buddha's "Fire Sermon," which is quoted in the notes of this study.[12] The reader who wishes to understand thoroughly the allusions and progression of this section should read it, Saint Augustine's *Confessions,* and Cantos XXVI-XXVII of Dante's *Purgatorio.* It will be seen that each of these focuses on the processes of escape from the total involvement in the life of the senses that we see reflected in the various scenes of misguided love suggested in *The Waste Land.* It is this broader reading of the word *lust* that is purged by Arnaut Daniel and by the speaker of *The Waste Land* in diving back into the fire of voluntary refinement.

In the third section the suggestions of improper love are at a further remove—seem less personally involved in the speaker's background. They are more mused upon than directly observed or relived. Mixed with these musings are the intimations of possible vitality inherent in Spenser's "Prothalamion," Shakespeare's *The Tempest,* and the voices of children in the choir loft of the Grail legends, presumably paralleled by the singing of the choir of angels or of the redeemed souls in Dante when another soul is redeemed from the barrenness of an improperly focused life. Yet the positive suggestions are not pure and unattenuated. The sound of horns and hunters which shall bring Actaeon to Diana in the spring becomes the noise of horns and motors that shall bring Sweeney to Mrs. Porter, a bawdyhouse madame; and the sacrament of foot-washing is perverted to Mrs. Porter and her daughter washing themselves in soda water ("And so they oughter, to keep 'em clean").

As already noted, the song of the nightingale is ambiguously present in this section, both in its pure sound "Twit twit twit" and in the "Jug jug jug jug jug jug" that is perverted to dirty ears. The dual significance, the juxtaposition of proper and improper loves, creates an effect that is "So rudely forc'd./Tereu." Next comes the poem's second "unreal city" passage, the recollection of the presumably homosexual overtures of Mr. Eugenides, the Smyrna merchant. This is followed by the seduction scene of the typist-home-at-teatime witnessed by Tiresias, who has foresuffered both male and female lusts and loves. The unperturbed if not unruffled typist, after the groping departure of the young man carbuncular, "smoothes her hair with automatic hand,/And puts a record on the gramophone." This arid suggestion of mechanical music is transmuted into the music of Ariel that crept by Ferdinand on the waters in *The Tempest*; it is associated with modern-London intimations of vitality, culminating in the "Inexplicable splendour of Ionian white and gold" of the church of Magnus Martyr.

Next come the songs of the three Thames-daughters, three London nymphs encountered by this modern Augustine-Aeneas when he first arrived in Boston-Paris-London-Carthage, to which he came "burning burning burning." But the corrosive fires of lust are modulated into the cleansing purgatorial fires of Saint Augustine and of Dante's Arnaut Daniel in the final "burning" which follows "O Lord Thou pluckest me out." This overt statement by the speaker of the poem signifies that he is being plucked out of the waste land to a new life of properly ordered love.

Section IV, "Death by Water," briefly summarizes what happens after the burial of the dead, improper life: "the cry of gulls and the deep sea swell/And the profit and loss" are forgotten. Phlebas, the drowned Phoenician sailor, passes "the stages of his age and youth/Entering the whirlpool"; and the reader is reminded that the same state awaits him—the dissolution of death which, if the good of the intellect is used, can result not in simple dissolution in fractured atoms "Beyond the circuit of the shuddering Bear" (*Gerontion*) but in the rebirth suggested by the many strands of allusion in this poem.

Section V, "What the Thunder Said," takes its title from the Second Brahmana passage on "The Three Cardinal Virtues," which is brief enough to be quoted in full:

1. The threefold offspring of Prajapati—gods, men, and devils (*asura*)—dwelt with their father Prajapati as students of sacred knowledge (*brahmacarya*).

Having lived the life of a student of sacred knowledge, the gods said: 'Speak to us, Sir.' To them he spoke this syllable, 'Da.' 'Did you understand?' 'We did understand,' said they. 'You said to us, "Restrain yourselves (*damyata*)."' 'Yes (*Om*)!' said he. 'You did understand.'

2. So then the men said to him: 'Speak to us, Sir.' To them then he spoke this syllable, 'Da.' 'Did you understand?' 'We did understand,' said they. 'You said to us, "Give (*datta*)."' 'Yes (*Om*)!' said he. 'You did understand.'

3. So then the devils said to him: 'Speak to us, Sir.' To them then he spoke this syllable, 'Da.' 'Did you understand?' 'We did understand,' said they. 'You said to us, "Be compassionate (*dayadhvam*)."' 'Yes (*Om*)!' said he. 'You did understand.'

This same thing does the divine voice here, thunder, repeat: *Da! Da! Da!* that is, restrain yourselves, give, be compassionate. One should practise this same triad: self-restraint, giving, compassion.[13]

In this fifth section of *The Waste Land* are given a number of analogous formulas for success in the quests of the poem's basic symbols. The first nine lines of the section place the themes in a Christian setting, putting us in Jerusalem just after the death of Christ and before his resurrection; the dryness and emptiness of this condition before rebirth is echoed in all of the patterns of the poem's various symbols. Here is the state of Gerontion, waiting for rain, being read to by a boy from the whole tradition, and looking back on his own renounced involvement in the life of attachment to the senses. As relief to the dry road winding among the mountains among rocks and in sand, without water, we have the mysterious figure who appeared to the disciples on the road to Emmaus, "the third who walks always beside you." For all ages, only when the life of temporal involvement is transcended, only when the towers and cities crumble as central psychic foci, only when the emptiness of the material and of man's pride in his accomplishments is seen, only when it is recognized that man's wells and cisterns are empty, can one approach the grail chapel, hear the crow of the cock seen in a flash of lightning on the rooftree, and feel the damp gust that brings the rain so long awaited.

Then in a jungle setting owing much to Conrad,[14] we hear the rumble of the thunder and the three commands Give, Sympathize, Control—each then related in turn to the speaker's own life and to works of literature which he has experienced. The final stanza of the poem returns to the Fisher King who is sitting on the shore fishing, with the arid plain behind him. He asks himself if he shall at least set his lands in order. Then follows a group of quoted fragments which he says "I have shored against my ruins." *Shore* here has the dual sense of *shoring up* and of pulling *to shore*.

The first fragment, from the children's rhyme "London Bridge Is Falling Down," suggests, perhaps, the decay of the bridge to the Grail castle; it also suggests positive values: the purity of the children who sing it, and the Fisher King's overcoming of attachment to the immediate life of the senses in his surroundings. The second, *"Poi s' ascose nel foco che gli affina,"* suggests Arnaut Daniel's eager and willing diving back into the cleansing fire which will prepare him to enter the Earthly Paradise. The third, *"Quando fiam uti chelidon"* ("When will I be like the swallow?") is from the *Pervigilium Veneris* and—like the next, "O swallow swallow" from Tennyson—indicates longing for successful rebirth that will follow the obeying of the three commands of the thunder. The next, *"Le Prince d'Aquitaine à la tour abolie,"* as Eliot's notes indicate, is from Gerard de Nerval's sonnet "El Desdichado," and it relates to the Grail myths with which de Nerval dramatically identified himself. It is the shoring of these fragments, as well as the method and content of the poem as a whole, that is referred to in the next quoted fragment, from Kyd's *Spanish Tragedy,* "Why then Ile fit you." This half-line repays closer examination than it has generally received, for it emerges as a key statement of Eliot's purpose in *The Waste Land*.

The line is striking in both works. In Kyd's play it is spoken by Hieronymo, Marshall of Spain, to the king's nephew Lorenzo and to Prince Balthazar of Portugal, the murderers of Hieronymo's son Horatio. In a war between their countries Balthazar, before the beginning of the play, had first killed Don Andrea, the lover of Bel-imperia, and then been defeated and captured by Horatio. When Bel-imperia then fell in love with Horatio, the envious Lorenzo and the lustful Balthazar treacherously murdered him. All this is secretly known to Hieronymo and Bel-imperia, but, since they dare not appeal to the villains' royal relatives for justice, they swear to help each other obtain revenge. At this juncture the murderers approach Hieronymo, who has previously entertained the court with a dumb show, to ask him a favor:

> LOR[enzo]. But now, Hieronymo, or never,
>   We are to entreat your help.
> HIER[onymo].   My help?
>   Why, my good lords, assure yourselves of me,
>   For you have given me cause—ay, by my faith,
>   have you!
> BAL[thazar]. It pleased you, at the entertainment of
>   the ambassador,
>   To grace the king so much as with a show.
>   Now were your study so well furnished,
>   As, for the passing of the first night's sport,
>   To entertain my father with the like,
>   Or any suchlike pleasing motion,
>   Assure yourself, it would content them well.
> HIER[onymo]. Is this all?
> BAL[thazar].   Ay, this is all.
> HIER[onymo]. Why then, I'll fit you; say no more.[15]

Hieronymo goes on to tell them that he has found again a tragedy he wrote when young, and he promises to present it if they will act in it, assuring them that "it will prove most passing strange, and wondrous plausible to that assembly." He relates the plot, which reproduces essentially, though not too obviously, the relationships existing among themselves. Each of the actors, he says, must speak his part in a different language so that the audience (chiefly their fathers) shall catch the true meaning of

the play. To Balthazar's protests that they will not be understood, the Marshall replies,

> It must be so, for the conclusion
> Shall prove the invention and all was good.
> And I myself in an oration,
> And with a strange and wondrous show besides,
> That I will have there behind a curtain
>   [the body of his murdered son, Horatio]
> Assure yourself, shall make the matter known.
> And all shall be concluded in one scene,
> For there's no pleasure ta'en in tediousness.

Like Hamlet, Hieronymo has feigned madness to avoid alert-
ing their fears; unsuspecting, they agree to humor him
("Hieronymo's mad againe") by acting the parts as he asks.
When they inquire who shall take the part of the murderer,
he replies, "O, that will I, my lords; make no doubt of it./I'll
play the murderer, I warrant you,/For I already have conceited
that." He carries out his promise to the letter when the play is
presented, murdering them on stage before their fathers' eyes;
and malevolently but heartbrokenly he reveals the true roles they
have played.

So in saying "Why then Ile fit you" (Eliot's version),
Hieronymo was saying not only "I'll supply your desire for
entertainment," but also "I'll adapt my techniques to your
circumstances," "I'll fit you into my intentions," "I'll alter my
play to fit our purposes," and "I'll provide what is fitting to
your deserts." And—the central theme of the play—Hieronymo,
by focusing his whole psyche on vengeance, has fitted himself
for the tortures of hell promised in the play's Epilogue. His
agonized and pitiless irony in the line borrowed by Eliot
epitomizes the psychic effect of revenge central to the tragedy
and etches itself indelibly on the reader's poetic sensibility.

Now let us see what Eliot has done with the line. He places
it at the end of a poem which has not only as its subject matter
but also as its form the processes of psychic progress. He is
presenting a literary work to a reader who probably expects
it to be roughly similar to many other poems he has read. The
poet knows, though, that the reader will find this poem largely
impervious to the usual approaches to poetry; he will be forced,
if he wishes to experience this poem, to adapt his efforts to the
form and techniques which Eliot has used. And in saying at

the poem's end "Why then Ile fit you," he is promising to fit the reader, through the poem and the patterns of experience necessary to the understanding of it, for possible success in his own quest.

Only by experiencing the works of art, literary and other, on which Eliot's poem draws, can the reader arrive at a truly comprehensive and detailed understanding of *The Waste Land* and achieve the state of the protagonist at the poem's end. The protagonist will fit the reader to put the Western traditions of literature, music, painting, architecture, and philosophy to what Eliot regards as their proper psychic or religious use. The poet-persona will provide entertainment, detective interest, and cultural instruction; but most importantly, he will help conduct the reader unawares down the hairy flank of Dante's Satan to that mysterious point at which he discovers that he is now climbing up toward the refining fire, having escaped his own waste land. The reader is reminded by this fragment that the aspiring psyche cannot focus on revenge or on the other dark lusts which separate it from other souls, but must dive eagerly into the refining flames.

What was in Kyd's play an impressive line has in *The Waste Land* entered fully into a new unity, and it has become a climactic statement of purpose which throws much light on the entire work. "Hieronymo's mad againe," the subtitle to an early edition of Kyd's play, seems here to indicate that Eliot, like Hieronymo, though he mixes languages and confounds some of the expectations of his audience, does so not out of madness nor lack of skill.

The Waste Land ends with the reiteration of the three commands of the thunder: Give, Sympathize, Control. The state that follows obedience to the commands is indicated by the "Shantih shantih shantih" of the last line, somewhat akin to the "Selah" with which some of our Psalms end, and translated by Eliot as "the peace that passeth understanding."

It is easy to see why Eliot denied that his poem was intended to express the disillusionment of a generation. Its message, though universal, is intensely personal; and the waste land exists in no one time or generation, but in a wrong psychic focus equally possible to all generations—and escapable, as our art reminds us, by individuals in every generation. What it is intended to express is the recognition not only of the anatomy of hell but of the necessity and promise of escape from it.

CHAPTER 5

Redeem the Dream

AS D. E. S. MAXWELL SUGGESTS, the waste land itself (not the poem) is "death's dream kingdom."[1] In *The Hollow Men*, this kingdom is contrasted with "death's other Kingdom" or "the twilight kingdom," which is the realm of Dante's earthly and heavenly paradises. This two-part division is based not on Dante's three canticles, but on the experience of the pilgrim in his relation to his lady Beatrice. The earthly paradise section of Dante's *Comedy* is indeed crucial to an understanding of either *The Hollow Men* or *Ash-Wednesday*: the meeting there with Beatrice is the turning point between the two kingdoms of death, and it is her eyes, or rather those of a lady analogous to her, that are feared and avoided, but desperately needed, in the "death's dream kingdom" of *The Hollow Men*. And to understand thoroughly the origins, motives, and emotional effects of that meeting, one must also know Dante's *Vita Nuova* (*The New Life*). To the objection that this demands too much of the reader, we can only reply that at least a dozen or so of the English poets commonly studied in undergraduate literature courses have assumed their readers to be familiar with those two works of Dante, and that most generations of English poetry readers have considered the demand neither unreasonable nor unprofitable.

Eliot speaks of "the system of Dante's organization of sensibility . . . the transition from Beatrice living to Beatrice dead, rising to the Cult of the Virgin. . . ."[2] It is in the *Vita Nuova* that we see Beatrice living and what she meant to Dante, who felt a voice within him, at their first meeting, cry, "Here beginneth the New Life." Beatrice, however, died early; and after her death, Dante was attracted to other loves. His affections strayed in various wrong directions until finally, in the middle of his life, he felt himself lost; or, as he says in the opening of the *Divine Comedy,* "I woke to find myself in a dark wood, where the right road was wholly lost and gone."

We find, however, in the *Divine Comedy,* that Beatrice, through love and pity for him, has sent Virgil to guide him through hell, where he will become aware of the nature of sin, and through purgatory to the earthly paradise, where he will meet her again. This is Beatrice dead, and she takes on greatly increased significance as intermediary between Dante and the highest love, the love of God. When Dante meets her there, he has already recognized in hell all that was debased in his former loves and inclinations; and in purgatory he has learned to turn away from the baser desires to the higher. In all this he was guided and counseled by Virgil and also, later, by Statius, who, unlike Virgil, was a Christian poet. Along the way these guides explained to Dante the nature of the soul and of love; but some things they could not explain. Beatrice, they promised, would be able to explain all such matters when he reached her.

The meeting between them, which takes place in cantos XXX and XXXI of *Purgatorio,* is crucially alluded to in both *The Hollow Men* and *Ash-Wednesday.* Since the parallels are much more detailed and complete in the latter, let us examine it first, and then indicate the relevance of the same materials to the slightly earlier poem, *The Hollow Men.* We must bear in mind, however, that *The Hollow Men* is a pivotal work; it pulls together strands from *Gerontion* and *The Waste Land,* the Sweeney poems and fragments, and the poetry of *Ash-Wednesday* and the *Four Quartets.* Probably the best procedure will be to discuss the six parts of *Ash-Wednesday* in order, and to clarify the links to Dante as they occur in Eliot's context; but first some introductory remarks are necessary.

I   Ash-Wednesday

In order of original publication, the parts of *Ash-Wednesday* are as follows: "Salutation" (1927, later Part II); "Perch'. io non spero" (1928, later Part I); "Al som de l'escalina" (1929, later Part III); Parts IV-VI added and the whole poem published under the title *Ash-Wednesday* (1930).

During the same period these works (as well as many others) appeared: "Lancelot Andrewes," *Journey of the Magi* (poem), *Shakespeare and the Stoicism of Seneca,* "Seneca in Elizabethan

Translation," "A Note on Poetry and Belief," "The Problems of the Shakespeare Sonnets" (review), "Poet and Saint" [Baudelaire] (review), "Popular Theologians" (review), "Archbishop Bramhall" (review), "Why Mr. Russell Is a Christian" (review), "The Twelfth Century" (review), *Fragment of an Agon* (dramatic poem), "The Mysticism of Blake" (review), "Bradley's 'Ethical Studies'," "Parliament and the New Prayer Book," *A Song for Simeon* (poem), *For Lancelot Andrewes, Dante, Animula* (poem), "The Devotional Poets of the Seventeenth Century: Donne, Herbert, Crashaw," "Mystic and Politician as Poet: Vaughan, Traherne, Marvell, Milton," "The Minor Metaphysicals: From Cowley to Dryden," "Religion without Humanism," "Essays of a Catholic Layman in England" (review), and "Christianity and Communism."

Clearly Eliot was very deeply involved with both religious and poetic questions, often overlapping each other. The fact that his poetry turned from the somewhat harsh negativity of Sweeney's world to the overtly religious topics of *The Hollow Men, Ash-Wednesday,* and the Ariel poems underscores this preoccupation. In 1927 Eliot had both joined the Church of England and become a British citizen, and we may assume that he participated in the church program of scripture study, which in each yearly course of the Christian calendar has one read the Psalms twelve times, the Old Testament once, and the New Testament twice. In such earlier works as *Mr. Eliot's Sunday Morning Service* (1918), *The Hippopotamus* (1917), and "Eeldrop and Appleplex" (1917), his concern with theology and with the proper functions and rituals of the church had already been apparent.

The strong focus on Dante in his writings during this period helps to explain why these elements combined as they did in *Ash-Wednesday*: Dante had used the liturgy, the Christian calendar, the scriptural lessons, and hymns integrally in the scheme of his *Divine Comedy*; and he had combined with them the concept of the poet's craft as a striving after the proper sort of love, a part of his path toward God, and, equally important, the role of Beatrice, mediating between earthly and heavenly love. When we combine with this Dantean example Eliot's preoccupation with Anglican bishops (Andrewes and Bramhall), devotional poets (Crashaw, Herbert, and Donne), and Church historians, many of the strands of *Ash-Wednesday* emerge quite naturally. A number of the statements by the speakers in Eliot's 1927 "A Dialogue on Dramatic Poetry" are relevant, including these:

> B: . . . We know too much, and are convinced of too little. Our literature is a substitute for religion, and so is our religion. . . .
>
> E: . . . I say that the consummation of the drama, the perfect and ideal drama, is to be found in the ceremony of the Mass. I say . . . that drama springs from religious liturgy, and that it cannot afford to depart far from religious liturgy. . . . But when drama has ranged as far as it has in our own day, is not the only solution to return to religious liturgy? And the only dramatic satisfaction that I find now is in a High Mass well performed. Have you not there everything necessary? And indeed, if you consider the ritual of the Church during the cycle of the year, you have the complete drama represented. The Mass is a small drama, having all the unities; but in the Church year you have represented the full drama of creation. . . .
>
> D: . . . The more fluid, the more chaotic the religious and ethical beliefs, the more the drama must tend in the direction of liturgy. Thus there would be some constant relation between drama and the religion of the time. . . .
>
> C: To sum up: there is no "relation" between poetry and drama. All poetry tends towards drama, and all drama towards poetry.[3]

Ash Wednesday, the first day of Lent, is a day of fasting, contrition, and self-denial in which the Anglican, the American Protestant Episcopalian, or the Catholic tries to renounce all other things and turn toward the things of God. Weeping and fasting accompany the repentance, and in the Ash Wednesday service of the Anglican *Book of Common Prayer*, various scriptural readings are assigned as follows: Morning Prayer—Psalms: 32, 143; First Lesson: Isaiah 58:1-12; Second Lesson: Hebrews 12:1-14. Evening Prayer—Psalms: 102, 130; First Lesson: Jonah 3 and 4; Second Lesson: Luke 15:11.

Much of Eliot's imagery comes directly from these scripture lessons, in which the themes of "turning" and "turning again," of bones and dryness, and of birds are repeated so often as to be inevitably associated with the topic of Ash Wednesday. One example should suffice: In the Jonah reading, the King of Nineveh, having been warned by the prophet, proclaims, ". . . let man and beast be covered with sackcloth, and cry mightily unto God: yea, let them turn every one from his evil way, and from the violence that is in their hands. Who can tell if God will turn and repent, and turn away from his fierce anger, that we perish not? And God saw their works, that they turned from their evil way; and God repented of the evil, that he had said that he would do unto them; and he did it not."

Naturally the biblical imagery, including that of "turning," has permeated the offices and liturgy of the Anglican Church. In the penitential office used on Ash Wednesday, we read, "O most mighty God, and merciful Father, who hast compassion upon all men, and who wouldest not the death of a sinner, but rather that he should turn from his sin, and be saved; Mercifully forgive us our trespasses. . . . Turn thou us, O good Lord, and so shall we be turned. Be favorable, O Lord, Be favorable to thy people, Who turn to thee in weeping, fasting, and praying. For thou art a merciful God. . . . Spare thy people, good Lord, spare them, And let not thine heritage be brought to confusion."

Eliot's poem also quotes other phrases from the liturgy—some of them biblical in origin—such as: "Pray to God to have mercy upon us"; "Pray for us sinners now and at the hour of our death"; "Lord, I am not worthy but speak the word only"; "And after this our exile"; and "O my people, what have I done unto thee." Moreover, since Dante drew on the same sources in the earthly paradise and the paradise sections of his *Divine Comedy*, familiarity with the scriptural lessons and with the liturgy of the Anglican Church will illuminate both Eliot's *Ash-Wednesday* and Dante's influence on it. Far from being a collection of six loosely related poems, *Ash-Wednesday* is, therefore, a disciplined expression of the experience of a particularly Dante-steeped penitent observing the Ash Wednesday rituals.

Another element from the traditions of the church that is heavily used by both Dante and Eliot is the imagery of what Eliot calls "the high dream"—the apocalyptic sort of imagery seen in the Book of Revelations, Daniel, Ezekiel, Isaiah; in Dante's earthly and heavenly paradises; and in the eagle and leopard imagery of *Ash-Wednesday*. This sort of imagery, though rare in twentieth-century poetry, is still very much alive in the ritual of the church; it is also alive in many widely known Negro spirituals. It is the imagery of the Mass, and it is the most natural vehicle for the poet—Christian or not—who wishes to depict one celebrating the religious mystery of the incarnation of primal love in human flesh. These are the proper concerns of an Ash-Wednesday penitent, and of the philosophical poets whom Eliot admires most—Dante, Lucretius, and the writers of the *Bhagavad-Gita*.

Were Eliot's poetry didactic in the derogatory sense of that word, nonCatholic and nonAnglican readers might at this point turn away from the poem. Fortunately, however, as a number of critics have pointed out, Eliot in even his most philosophical and most religious poetry is setting before the reader authentic human experience—states, psychic actions, and realizations rather than labels and logical formulations. In this characteristic he may again be said to resemble Dante, who can be read with enjoyment and profit by a reader who rejects his theology, or who at least has reservations regarding it. Even in this most Christian of his poems, there is nothing narrow about Eliot's use of Christian symbols—indeed, he takes care to suggest through non-Christian symbols that the experience dealt with is paralleled outside the Christian persuasion.

To the objection that the diction is too exclusively Christian, we can only answer that, to represent the experience with which the poem deals, an artist in our culture perhaps can turn to no other satisfactory body of symbols—though *The Waste Land* may be cited to partially refute that statement. Since Christian symbolism is the most consistent body of symbolism built into our culture that is relevant to the psychic patterns which *Ash-Wednesday* celebrates, an artist of Eliot's abilities and intentions could turn to no other symbols in examining the whole question of artistic symbolism and artistic responsibility. To state it differently, we might say that a given time and place is likely to offer the artist only one vocabulary in which to express the relations between genuinely religious content and the problems of the artist.

Not surprisingly, the solutions to the chief critical problems of the poem are related to, and grow out of, the lines most likely to be noticed and questioned at a first reading—such lines as "Lady, three white leopards sat under a juniper-tree"; "Who walked between the violet and the violet"; "Because these wings are no longer wings to fly/But merely vans to beat the air"; "Till the wind shake a thousand whispers from the yew"; "But when the voices shaken from the yew-tree drift away/Let the other yew be shaken and reply"; and "While jewelled unicorns draw by the gilded hearse." And every one of these is greatly clarified by echoes from Dante, to whom we shall refer as we analyze the various sections of the poem.

Part I ("Perch' io non spero")

Both the title "Perch' io non spero" and its translation in the first line, "Because I do not hope to turn again," in Part I derive from a poem by Guido Cavalcanti (the friend to whom Dante dedicated his *Vita Nuova*), a *ballata* written in exile to Cavalcanti's Lady, whom he did not expect to see again before dying. Since the conception of the Lady seen in the *ballata* derives from the courtly love tradition of the Provençal troubadors via the Sicilian and Tuscan schools of Italian poetry—to which Dante, Cavalcanti, Pistoia, and other advocates of their "sweet new style" added the worship of the Virgin Mary—this *ballata* implies a relinquishing of aspirations toward both Cavalcanti's Lady and his poetic craft, of which she is the muse. The poem is also relevant to *Ash-Wednesday* in a number of other ways: It is directed to carry tidings of sighs, tidings full of pain and gentle fear, to the Lady; but it must use discretion lest it come into the hands of someone hostile to a gentle nature, which would bring to the poet both reproof by the Lady and agony, weeping, and grief after death. The poet says, "so much of my being is destroyed already, that I can suffer no more," and he urges the poem to adore his Lady forever and tell her of his sufferings. His renunciation, like that in Part I of *Ash-Wednesday*, suggests the state of Dante after the death of Beatrice; and perhaps it gives added significance to Eliot's dedication of his poem to the first Mrs. Eliot. The "Perch' io non spero" line recurs near the end of Part I and again, with a slight change, at the beginning of Part VI.

Part I of *Ash-Wednesday* contains at least five triads of various sorts. The first three stanzas, each beginning "Because I . . . ," comprise one of the triads; and they are summarized in the couplet "Consequently I rejoice, having to construct something/ Upon which to rejoice." Line four rejects "Desiring this man's gift and that man's scope." This easily recognized echo from Shakespeare's Sonnet 29 ("When in disgrace with fortune and men's eyes . . ."), one noted by a number of critics, will remind readers familiar with Eliot's book *Dante* that in it the author compared Shakespeare and Dante; he generously divided the mount of Parnassus between them, and concluded "There is no third." He also suggested that the comparison of the *Vita Nuova* with Shakespeare's sonnets would be an interesting occupation, and in 1927 he had reviewed J. M. Robertson's

The Problems of Shakespeare's Sonnets. Coupled with the many links to the *Vita Nuova* in *Ash-Wednesday*, these suggestions should soon lead the reader to notice that the Part II references to the organs eaten by the leopards—"my heart my liver and that which had been contained/In the hollow round of my skull"—correspond to the seats of the three spirits that make up Dante's identity in his moving description of the effects of his first meeting with Beatrice at the age of nine. The passages containing these, rearranged to match the order of the first three lines of *Ash-Wednesday*, as I read them, are as follows:

NATURAL SPIRIT   SEAT: LIVER

"At that moment the natural spirit, which dwelleth there where our nourishment is administered, began to weep, and in weeping said these words: *Heu Miser! Quia frequenter impeditus ero deinceps.* (Alas! How often shall I be disturbed from this time forth.)"

SPIRIT OF LIFE   SEAT: HEART

"At that moment, I say most truly that the spirit of life, which hath its dwelling in the secretest chamber of the heart, began to tremble so violently . . . it said these words: *Ecce deus fortior me, qui veniens dominabitur mihi.* (Here is a deity stronger than I; who, coming, shall rule over me.)"

ANIMATE SPIRIT   SEAT: BRAIN

"At that moment the animate spirit, which dwelleth in the lofty chamber whither all the senses carry their perceptions, was filled with wonder, and speaking more especially to the spirits of the eyes, said these words: *Apparuit jam beatitude vestra.* (Your beatitude hath now been made manifest unto you.)"[4]

So the three sorts of striving renounced in Part I seem to be the diets of the three leopards in Part II, of whom more will be said shortly; and in the sets of triads already mentioned, each contains elements relatable to the three spirits. How far the parallel should be pushed is open to question, but I would hazard the following identifications in Part I: Natural Spirit— striving for the physical attainment of the earthly Lady, "hope to turn again," "infirm glory of the positive hour," "the blessèd face," "having to construct something/Upon which to rejoice," and "The air which is now thoroughly small and dry"; Spirit of Life—striving of the conscious will, "hope," "Because I do not

think," "I rejoice that things are as they are," "And pray to God
to have mercy upon us," and "Smaller and dryer than the will";
Animate Spirit—striving of the poet-prophet, "hope to turn/
Desiring this man's gift . . .," "I cannot drink/There . . .," "And
renounce the voice," "matters that with myself I too much
discuss," and "these wings."

In renouncing the poet-prophet's striving, the protagonist
compares himself to an aged eagle (the eagle was known to
Dante and to his contemporaries as the bird that could look at
the sun without being blinded, as the poet can look at the truth
more steadily than most of his fellows). The transition from
Beatrice living to Beatrice dead fuses the three sorts of renunciation, and at any rate the three spirits are not separable except
as an expedient of analysis: In the poem, as in life, they merge
and intertwine.

Dante's *Vita Nuova* and *Divine Comedy* study the journey
from earthly love to the highest felicity in the attainment of
the deified Lady, and the use in Eliot's earlier poetry of
purgatorial symbolism—along with such symbols as Tristan
and Isolde and the Holy Grail—may be taken to indicate an
earlier, more optimistic period in which the poet felt greater
faith in his art as a means of attaining such felicity. Now, however, he knows "that time is always time/And that place is
always and only place/And what is actual is actual only for one
time/And only for one place." Such aspirations are possible only
for one place and one time, for Dante in 1300, perhaps again
in one time and one place for himself or some other poet, but
not with any sense of permanence. And as Eliot says later in
East Coker,

> And what there is to conquer
> By strength and submission, has already been discovered
> Once or twice, or several times, by men whom one can
> not hope
> To emulate—but there is no competition—
> There is only the fight to recover what has been lost
> And found and lost again and again: and now, under
> conditions
> That seem unpropitious. . . .

Since this is true, he says, "Consequently I rejoice, having to
construct something/Upon which to rejoice/And pray to God
to have mercy upon us." Such efforts and such confident aspira-

tions as were seen in the earlier poetic attempts form a proper stage in the artist's development ("The vanished power of the usual reign"); but they cannot be permanent, "Because one has only learnt to get the better of words/For the thing one no longer has to say, or the way in which/One is no longer disposed to say it." Realizing all this, and aiming toward the acceptance, the relaxed and humble acceptance of his proper place in the scheme of things, the poet in *Ash-Wednesday* prays for mercy and says, "Let these words answer/For what is done, not to be done again/May the judgement not be too heavy upon us." And because his will and his craft are no longer seen as wings to fly, because he realizes it is not by his own concentration and exertion of will that the proper state can be reached, he prays, "Teach us to care and not to care/Teach us to sit still."

And as discussed earlier, the Dantean psychology implicit in the entire body of Eliot's poetry underlies the need to request prayer "now and at the hour of our death," in order that we may make now the proper choices that will make the moment after death one that can be aided by prayer. Thus the state suggested by this first section of *Ash-Wednesday* is one of deep humility growing out of an awareness of one's actual and one's proper relation to the universe. The turning away of all three renunciations symbolizes the turning to God which permeates the scriptures and liturgy traditionally connected with Ash Wednesday, and the protagonist does not hope to turn again away from God to a reliance in himself and his capacities. This is the authentic state of the celebrant of the Ash Wednesday rituals and meditations.

Part II ("Salutation")

Eliot's emphasis on questions of the proper roles of the artist and of artistic aspiration is further seen in the epigraph originally attached to Part II: "The Hand of the Lord Was Upon Me:—*e vo significando*." The Italian clause occurs in the passage of *Purgatorio* XXIV in which Dante explains to the poet Bonagiunta of Lucca his "sweet new style (*dolce stil nuovo*)": "'I am one who, when Love inspires me take note, and go setting it forth after the fashion which he dictates within me.'"[5] Both the sense of the passage and the explicit references in the context relate it to the *Vita Nuova*, which, like the *Divine Comedy*, makes it clear that the love which inspires the poet stands not only for the earthly love of the Lady, but also for the higher love of the Virgin, of whom she is a figure, and also for the final love of God, which is figured in both of them.[6] Dante's passage occurs on the sixth cornice of purgatory in a context highly relevant to *Ash-Wednesday*, between the encounters with the two yew trees of that cornice, both scions of the Tree of Knowledge, "thus linking up the Sin of Gluttony with the sin of Eve and the Fall of Man."[7] Bonagiunta replies to Dante: " 'Oh brother,' said he, 'now I see the knot which kept back the Notary, and Guittone, and me, short of the sweet new style that I hear. Truly I see how your pens follow close after him who dictates, which certainly befell not with ours.' "

The first half of the epigraph comes from the dry bones passage of Ezekiel 37, and it ushers in the imagery of the higher dream, of bones and leopards and Ladies (as of the eagle in Part I). Eliot applied the term "high dream" to the divine pageant accompanying the appearance of Beatrice in Dante's earthly paradise, and its strict parallel in *Ash-Wednesday* is in the line "While jewelled unicorns draw by the gilded hearse." He also linked it to "the serious pageants of royalty, of the church, of military funerals," and both he and Dante are here echoing the pageant of the Mass—in which the protagonist of Eliot's poem is participating. We may compare Beatrice's speech to Dante in *Paradiso* IV: "Needs must such speech address your faculty, which only from the sense-reported thing doth apprehend what it then proceedeth to make fit matter for the intellect. And therefore doth the Scripture condescend to your capacity, assigning foot and hand to God, with other meaning; and Holy Church doth represent to you with human aspect Gabriel and Michael, and him too who made Tobit sound again [Raphael]."[8]

So Eliot's epigraph attests the faithfulness of the heightened imagery to the poet's inspiration, as well as his submissiveness, and also the relevance to this section of the love of the Lady in all her ramifications. He is claiming for his poem the highest inspiration, derived from the ultimate, the Primal Love.

The humility and submission of Part I is equated to the dry bones lying in the sand and scattered. The value of the renunciation is suggested in the brightness of the bones, the result of the goodness of the Lady. The leopards who fed to satiety on the three spirits of the protagonist suggest the beasts (leopard, lion, and wolf) who menaced Dante at the beginning of his journey, the leopard being identified in the Temple Classics notes with worldly pleasure. Dorothy Sayers throws light on both the nature of the imagery and the identity of this beast when she says that "the soul's cherished sins have become, as it were, externalized, and appear to it like demons or 'beasts' with a will and a power of their own, blocking all progress. Once lost in the Dark Wood, a man can only escape by so descending into himself that he sees his sin, not as an external obstacle, but as the will to chaos and death within him (Hell)."[9] This seems a fair description of Eliot's *Ash-Wednesday* leopards.

The juniper tree under which the leopards sat suggests the juniper under which Elijah sat in I Kings 19: Having overcome and slain the priests of Baal, Elijah has been forced by Jezebel's threats to flee into the wilderness. He sits under the tree and implores, "Now, O Lord, take away my life; for I am not better than my fathers." His attitude is similar to that of the penitent of our poem, and further details suggest the forty-day Lenten season, the communion, and the final vision of God: He falls asleep and is twice wakened by an angel who commands him to eat of a cake baked there on coals and to drink from a cruse of water. This sacrament sustains him through forty days spent on Mount Horeb, the mount of God, without further nourishment. Finally, after a strong wind that breaks the rocks, an earthquake, and a fire, God reveals himself in a still small voice telling the prophet to go and anoint not only new kings over Syria and Israel but also a new prophet to take his own place.[10] As in the Ezekiel account, God asks, "Shall these bones live?" There He commanded Ezekiel to prophesy to the bones and promised to reassemble them and clothe them in flesh, make them live again, and place them in the land of their inheritance according to His previous promises. "That which had been contained/In the bones" replies, chirping with the burden of the grasshopper of Ecclesiastes 12, a passage also relevant to *Gerontion* and *The Waste Land*:

> Remember now thy Creator in the days of thy youth, while the evil days come not, nor the years draw nigh, when thou shalt say, I have no pleasure in them. . . . And the doors shall be shut in the streets, when the sound of the grinding is low, and he shall rise up at the voice of the bird . . . and the almond tree shall flourish, and *the grasshopper* [my italics] shall be a burden, and desire shall fail: because man goeth to his long

home, and the mourners go about the streets. . . . And moreover, because the preacher was wise, he still taught the people knowledge. . . . The preacher sought to find out acceptable words . . . even words of truth. . . . And further, by these, my son, be admonished: of making many books there is no end; and much study is a weariness of the flesh. Let us hear the conclusion of the whole matter: Fear God, and keep his commandments: for this is the whole duty of man.

"The burden of the grasshopper" comprises the chief strands of meaning of *Ash-Wednesday*, Part I.

The conscious striving that has been disavowed was a poetic striving, a prophesying. The poet has God say, "Prophesy to the wind, to the wind only for only/The wind will listen." The protagonist proffers his deeds to oblivion (as Jonah was reluctant to do in the Jonah 4, Ash-Wednesday scripture lesson), and this compliance recovers those parts of him which the leopards reject. The song of the bones is addressed to the Virgin Mary and is patterned on Saint Bernard's prayer to her in Cantos XXXII and XXXIII of the *Paradiso*. Beatrice, in that context, has served to the limits of her usefulness for Dante's aspirations; and she has been replaced by Saint Bernard, more qualified by virtue of his contemplative life, to direct Dante's attention far beyond where they stand to the Holy Virgin, the Queen of Heaven.

Dante's vision has in several successive steps been dazzled and gradually adapted to the brighter loves encountered throughout his journey: first from the dark pestilence of hell to the dawn of Mount Purgatory, then to the circling sun, the guardian angels, the divine pageant of the earthly paradise, and the eyes of Beatrice; then through the various degrees of the seven heavens. Each of these steps has been comparable to the readjustment of vision in Plato's "Allegory of the Cave." Now Dante is gazing on the multifoliate rose of the whole company of the blest, the Church Triumphant. Dante has been made aware of the symbolic nature of much that he has seen. In order that he might understand, he encountered the various shades in various heavens; yet in these final cantos they all are in the multifoliate rose, at the limits of his present heightened ability to comprehend. And now, that he may re-expand his vision and gaze directly on the felicity of Mary, Bernard directs his attention upward. As Dante warms to the intense love that radiates from her and is

mirrored all round by the blessed souls, Bernard prays to her to
fit Dante to look directly on the vision of God, the Primal Love.

BERNARD'S PRAYER

Virgin mother,
daughter of thy son,
lowly and uplifted
more than any other creature,
fixed goal of the eternal counsel,

. . . .

ASH-WEDNESDAY PRAYER

Lady of silences
Calm and distressed
Torn and most whole
Rose of memory
Rose of forgetfulness

. . . .

Bernard's prayer is answered, and the *Divine Comedy* closes on
Dante's attempt to dimly figure the vision of the Primal Love
then revealed to him—"the highest point that poetry has ever
reached or ever can reach."

Part II of *Ash-Wednesday* closes with the bones singing
"We are glad to be scattered, we did little good to each other"
and with their acceptance of dryness and separation as the
land of their inheritance, according to the adjusted vision of the
higher dream.

Part III ("*Som de l'escalina*")

The title "Som de l'escalina," originally attached to Part III,
refocuses our attention on the late cantos of *Purgatorio*, specifically on the exchange between Dante and Arnaut Daniel, already
referred to in Chapter 4. It is Arnaut who, in the lines most
often used by Eliot, asks to be remembered when Dante reaches
"the topmost of the stair." "Sovegna vos" ("Be mindful [in due
time of my pain]")—from the same speech—will appear shortly
in Part IV of *Ash-Wednesday*.

This title identifies the vantage point from which the penitent's
"blind eye" recreates in Part III the climbing of the three stairs
whose identification has given critics some difficulty. Certainly

a purgational process is there symbolized—a process having parallels in the major divisions of the *Divine Comedy,* in the divisions of the *Purgatorio,* and in the stairs used as a figure of mystical progress in the writings of Saint John of the Cross and of various other Christian and non-Christian mystics. But Eliot's references to such precise points as "the first turning of the second stair," "the second turning of the second stair," and "the first turning of the third stair" show clearly that he had highly specific intentions for this imagery. These stairs seem to have two close echoes in Dante: the three steps of penitence—*confession, contrition,* and *satisfaction*—and the three classes of improperly ordered love on which the structure of purgatory is based—*distorted, defective,* and *excessive* loves.[11] Their immediate source is probably in the three steps to the high altar and the turnings of the Mass ceremony.

At any rate, in Dantean terms the three strophes of Part III of *Ash-Wednesday* bring the protagonist almost to the top of the stairs, to the point at which he is about to make the passage to the earthly paradise—or to partake of the sacrament of the Mass. Having almost completed the purgation of his improperly ordered loves, he is nearing the top of the third stair; he looks back and remembers the process by which he has come to this point; and at this moment his faith and humility are expressed in the line from the Mass, taken from Matthew 8:8, "Lord, I am not worthy but speak the word only." This "word" suggests the words of the angels who admit Dante and his companions to each cornice of purgatory, without which none can proceed. Whoever is admitted to the last stair has disciplined his appetites and ordered his loves; he has reached a condition in which his own inclinations are the surest guides to proper conduct.

The third stair seems to involve the purgation of excessive love: of avarice, gluttony, and lust. Certainly the imagery of the third strophe is highly sexual, with its slotted window, hawthorn blossom, broadbacked figure dressed in blue and green playing an antique flute, blown hair, lilac and brown hair. However, these distraction themes, these unwilling memories, are fading; and the protagonist experiences a strength beyond hope and despair, a strength which allows him to resign himself, accepting rather than willing, preparing himself for the entry to the earthly paradise—to life at its best on this earth. I would suggest that Eliot's poem does not exclude what C. S. Lewis, in *The Allegory of Love,* refers to as "a love which reaches the divine without abandoning the human and becomes spiritual while remaining carnal also."[12] However, the death of Beatrice in the *Vita Nuova* and Dante's exile suggest reasons for Dante's eschewing such a solution; and Eliot's protagonist presumably has similar reasons for renouncing the blessed face. Speculations as to what might have been had Beatrice lived longer are fruitless in this context.

The seeming regression of Part III from the paradisal echoes of Bernard's "Queen of Heaven" prayer in Part II clarifies the protagonist's subtle awareness of the levels of symbolism and imagery that are part of his poet-penitent quest for felicity: Only symbolically has he experienced what Dante is talking about in the end of *Paradiso,* and the disposition to regard the poetic conception as real rather than symbolic is perhaps the form of gluttony that detains Forese, Bonagiunta of Lucca, and our protagonist on the sixth cornice of purgatory for a time—an excessive savoring of the involvement in the sensual aspects of the craft of poetry. The surrendering of "word" for "Word" is one of the most difficult renunciations for the poet.

Part IV

Cantos XXVIII to XXXIII of *Purgatorio* will shed more light on the sequence of developments in Part IV than any amount of comment, and should be read with it.

The first eleven lines of Part IV are another prayer, another salutation, and every line of this section evokes echoes of Dante. On reaching Canto XXVII, Eliot wrote in his essay "Dante": "we have left behind the stage of punishment and the stage of dialectic, and approach the state of Paradise. The last cantos have the quality of the *Paradiso* and prepare us for it."[13] It is these sections that are important to *Ash-Wednesday.* Part IV, despite its various levels of imagery, seems to me an intensely personal utterance. As the sacramental elements of the Mass, covered with a fine white cloth (compare "wearing/White light folded, sheathed about her, folded"), are about to be revealed, the penitent is contemplating the whole scale of his own symbols related to this symbol of Primal Love. He is considering his own history and the role played in it by a figure closely analogous to Beatrice as she is seen from the *Vita Nuova* to near the end of *Paradiso.* As now contemplated, she suggests the Beatrice of *Purgatorio* XXX, Dante's parallel to the sacramental elements of the Mass. As Dorothy Sayers says, "To the penitent and purified soul the God-bearing Image (whatever it may be) appears, accompanied by its whole train of functionaries; but that vision is unique and personal to every man that sees it. For Dante, the Image is Beatrice whose handmaid is Matilda; for others, other Images will doubtless perform the like offices."[14]

The prayer beginning Part IV is a plea for remembrance to the Lady or Ladies who are the referent of the pronoun "Who" used in four of those lines. The referent has been variously interpreted; one critic even makes it interrogative. It appears, however, that all of the female God-bearing figures are included in this salutation, including Dante's Matilda, Beatrice, Mary, and the protagonist's own unnamed God-bearing figures. The symbols of Part IV certainly combine his personal symbols with the full range of meanings of the Lady for Dante and for Cavalcanti. For specific references, we may compare Dante's progress in the earthly paradise.

Entering the sacred wood, walking beneath the trees from which the birds sing down, Dante approaches the clear stream of Lethe. Beyond it, he sees a happy Lady, Matilda. Eliot's first line, "Who walked between the violet and the violet," suggests either Beatrice as we shall see her shortly or Matilda, "who went singing and plucking flower after flower, wherewith her path was pied"; for Eliot's penitent it may also suggest the continuum from "the lost lilac" or "the violet hour" of the seduction scene in *The Waste Land* to the violet hour of "the dreamcrossed twilight" "between the last blue rocks," from the earliest and lowest forms of earthly love to the higher love of innocence symbolized in Matilda and Beatrice.

After Matilda has explained the nature of the earthly paradise to Dante—that it is the Garden of Eden from which Eve caused man to be banished—the divine pageant approaches; some of the figures in this pageant are dressed in green, and the four apocalyptic beasts are crowned with green leaves. Hope, one of the theological virtues, is naturally green. Eliot's "The various ranks of varied green" may also refer to the foliage of the sacred wood. The procession also provides a possible referent for "between the violet and the violet," since the four cardinal virtues of prudence, justice, temperance, and fortitude are clothed in purple, and it is Beatrice who appears between these various figures. Beatrice herself wears a crown of olive over a white veil and under a green mantle is clad in the hue of living flame.

This emphasis on the color of her garments in both *Purgatorio* and *Ash-Wednesday* echoes the *Vita Nuova* passage in which Dante vividly recalls the red gown in which Beatrice first appeared to him at the age of nine. In the earthly paradise, Dante— on seeing the veiled Beatrice (even though he has not yet recognized her)—is deeply shaken by "the tokens of the ancient flame"; he turns to Virgil, only to find him gone. When he starts to weep over Virgil's loss, Beatrice addresses him: "Dante, . . . weep not yet, for soon another sword shall give thee cause to weep." This is the only time Dante's name appears in the *Divine Comedy*. Beatrice then identifies herself (though still veiled), and she accuses him of having strayed from his love for her and of having succumbed to the temptation of the sirens. Confessing with great difficulty, he succumbs to a bright cloud of tears. The bird and wing imagery of Part I is suggested by her rebuke: " 'Young damsel or other vain thing with so brief enjoyment, should not have weighed down thy wings to await more shots. The young bird waits two or three, but before the eyes of the full-fledged in vain the net is spread or arrow shot.' "[15]

Dante's remorse and repentance make him stand with downcast eyes like a scolded child until she forces him to hold up his head and look at her. Her great beauty makes him swoon, and when he regains consciousness he has been plunged into Lethe by Matilda. The relevance of baptism and its recovenanting in absolution is obvious. Having drunk of Lethe's waters, he is led out on the other side by the four cardinal virtues, who promise, "We'll lead thee to her eyes . . . the orbs of emerald/ Whence love let fly his former shafts at thee." As he looks on Beatrice's eyes and satisfies his ten-year thirst, he sees reflected in her eyes the griffon who represents Christ in the pageant, for her gaze is fixed on it. So she is already directing Dante's attention to the Word.

Another masque-like scene follows involving the figures in the divine pageant and the Tree of Knowledge, of which the two yews of cornice six are scions. Afterwards, Beatrice places the seven virtues in front of her; and, without speaking, she, with merely a nod, beckons to Dante, Matilda, and Statius to follow her. It is then that she partly explains the pageant, but she also tells Dante that her explanation surpasses his understanding in order that he might recognize the limitations of his own powers and knowledge and see the difference between the divine way and earthly ways. They proceed to the stream Eunoe, where Dante drinks the draught that makes him remember all good things in his experience, and he comes back "pure and ready to mount to the stars" (end of Canto XXXIII).

So in Part IV of *Ash-Wednesday* the protagonist is experiencing through Dante's art a symbolic redemption toward which he aspires in his own time and place; but he is still in the years that walk between:

> Here are the years that walk between, bearing
> Away the fiddles and the flutes, restoring
> One who moves in the time between sleep and waking, wearing
> White light folded, sheathed about her, folded.

Eliot is restoring with a new verse—his own—the ancient rhyme of Dante; he is also restoring with the new heavenly verse—the higher dream—the ancient earthly love. The Ash-Wednesday penitent is aspiring to Dante's experience and is praying to his God-bearing figures for their favorable attention and help. He is still, as we will learn in Part VI, "wavering between the profit and the loss," near the top of Mount Purgatory; but he has not yet drunk of Lethe, which will enable him to forget "These matters that with myself I too much discuss/Too much explain." He hopes to redeem not only the time but also the dream which he has read in Dante and which is implied in his God-bearing figures—which are, like Beatrice, the token of the Church, of the Word, of Christ, and of Primal Love. But that Word is "unheard, unspoken/Till the wind shake a thousand whispers from the yew" (in *Purgatorio* XXXII such sweet music comes from the Tree of Knowledge that Dante cannot bear it and falls asleep; "human kind/Cannot bear very much reality," as we are told in *Burnt Norton*). And after the whispers from the yew, then the Incarnate Word will be shown to him in the eyes of the Lady.

Part IV concludes with the reminder, from the "Salve Regina" of the liturgy, that Mary stands as a link to the Word, the divine image, which shall follow: "Turn then, most gracious advocate, thine eyes of mercy towards us. And after this our exile, show unto us the blessed fruit of thy womb, Jesus."[16] Eliot uses only the line "And after this our exile."

Part V

Part V of *Ash-Wednesday* begins with the well-known incantatory consideration of the Word, culminating in the lines "Against the Word the unstilled world still whirled/ About the centre of the silent Word," and continuing in the next strophe in the self-aware but not self-conscious "Where shall the word be found, where will the word/Resound?" passage. Such echoing and balancing of tensions is carried on throughout Part V, a section which seems to owe more than just a text to the sonorous sermons of Lancelot Andrewes.

That text of the Word or Logos has been used frequently in Eliot's poetic career: as "The word within a word, unable to speak a word,/Swaddled with darkness" in *Gerontion* (1920); as "In the beginning was the Word./Superfetation of *to en*" in *Mr. Eliot's Sunday Morning Service* (1918), implying the Greek origins in Heraclitus and before; as the present passage in *Ash-Wednesday* and "the Infant, the still unspeaking and unspoken Word" of *A Song for Simeon* (1928); in *The Rock* as "Knowledge of words and ignorance of the Word" and "Where the word is unspoken/We will build with new speech" in Chorus I, "Much is your reading, but not the Word of God" and "the time-kept City; where My Word is unspoken" in Chorus III, and "Then it seemed as if men must proceed from light to light, in the light of the Word [after the Incarnation]" in Chorus VII.

And finally, in *Burnt Norton,* appears "The Word in the desert," as well as the Greek epigraph from the Logos passage of Heraclitus that reads as follows: "This Word [Logos] is from everlasting, yet men understand it as little after the first hearing of it as before. For though all things come to pass according to this Word, men seem wanting in experience when they examine the words and deeds I set forth, distinguishing each thing in its nature and showing how it truly is. But other men know not what they do when awake, even as they forget what they do in sleep. . . ."[17] The Gospel of John opens with a newer version: "In the beginning was the Word, and the Word was with God, and the Word was God. The same was in the beginning with God. All things were made by him; and without him was not anything made that was made. In him was life; and the life was the light of men." Lancelot Andrewes may very well be responsible for this King James version of John. (He was one of the committee of translators.) At any rate it is echoed in the sermon from which Eliot quotes the lines "The word within a word, unable to speak a word," which he calls an example of Andrewes' "flashing phrases which never desert the memory."[18]

Eliot's Word passage at the beginning of Part V of *Ash-Wednesday* closes with the suggestion of the profound re-orientation achieved by Dante in *Paradiso* when he realized that what had seemed to him the farthest and widest sphere was really the still center of the universe, with the discordant, unstilled world whirling about it at a great distance. But "For those who walk in darkness . . . who avoid the face," conditions for finding the Word are not propitious, we are told in the next strophe. Eliot's veiled sister, the Beatrice figure, is asked to pray for those about to partake of the divine revelation, those about to spit from the mouth the withered apple seed, the last vestige of Eve's guilt in eating of the Tree of Knowledge and of Persephone's partaking of the pomegranate in the underworld— both of which are explained by Dante's Matilda as relevant to the earthly paradise. This emptying of the mouth suggests the whole pattern of confession, contrition, and satisfaction which prepares the Ash-Wednesday communicant to take in his mouth the sacred Elements—now already revealed on the altar.

The two earlier repetitions of the Good Friday Reproach, "O my people, what have I done unto thee," spoken by God to his rebellious people in Micah 6:3, suggest the difficulty in the whirling world of proper orientation to the Word, as well as the undeservedness of Christ's rejection by men. In the Micah passage, God enumerates the blessings He has given and concludes, "O my people, remember now . . . that ye may know the righteousness of the Lord." It is this positive note that is suggested by the "O my people" that concludes Part V.

The "word" of this part of the poem is not only the divine Word but also the poetic word. It is only in Dante's poetry that the final meeting with the Lady leads to the unattenuated vision of Primal Love. It is only in poetry or after death that the felicity depicted by Dante can be achieved. The vision of Dante is good only for one time and one place, and, though the protagonist of *Ash-Wednesday* has chosen the veiled sister, he is terrified and cannot surrender; he affirms before the world and denies between the rocks—the last blue rocks of Part V, which suggest the stairway to the earthly paradise on which Dante, Virgil, and Statius spend the night after the dark shadows have closed in around them. On the next morning comes the long-desired reunion.

Part VI

The opening of Part VI, substituting "Although" for "Because," surrenders even the causal emphasis of "Perch' io non spero." Again "I do not hope" is repeated three times, reminding us of the three spirits renounced and of the protagonist's inability to correct his own state. Here he wavers in the twilight between birth and dying, the years which, he hopes, are bearing away the sensuous attachment to earthly things—attachment to lesser loves. It is also the dreamcrossed twilight between the dying out of the renounced appetites and the spiritual birth hoped to be ahead. In this ambivalent state he asks for the blessing of the priest ("Bless me father"); and he confesses that, although he does not wish it, the images of the rejected objects of the appetites, of the unordered loves, still recur to him. Still "the lost heart stiffens" and "the blind eye creates/The empty forms between the ivory gates." But the nearness of success is indicated: these are *empty* forms, seen at the ivory gates from which, as in Virgil's *Aeneid,* the *false* dreams issue. The rocks of this place are "blue of Mary's colour," the color of grace.

The three dreams that cross in this purple twilight reiterate the three rejected spirits, the leopards, and the stairs; they further echo Oedipus' "place where three roads meet" and Plato's similar references in the myth of the soul's experiences after death in the *Phaedo.* The yew tree references suggest *Purgatorio* XXXII and the unbearably sweet singing from the Tree of Knowledge, of Man's proper nature after Christ the griffon has reunited to the Tree the chariot pole (his cross, traditionally of yew wood).

The penitent has seen the anatomy of hell, has recognized the nature of his improper impulses; he has heard the voices crying examples of temperance and gluttony from the two yews of cornice six, where his poet-acquaintances purge the excessive attachment to the life of the senses that seems almost an occupational hazard for them. His struggle is not to be won unequivocally before death, but it can be won through the humility and acceptance of Ash Wednesday and through the grace figured in the Ladies, to whom the final prayer of the poem is offered. "Our peace in His will" ("*e la sua volontate é nostra pace"*) was spoken by Piccarda de Donati in Dante's *Paradiso* III as she explained that though there are degrees of blessedness in heaven, each spirit there accepts his own place without jealousy or discontent. *Ash-Wednesday* closes with the prayer that immediately precedes the receiving of the Eucharist, "Suffer me not to be separated/And let my cry come unto Thee."

It will be found on reflection that the main differences between *Ash-Wednesday* and *The Waste Land* are in the exclusiveness of the Christian imagery used and in the degree of self-revelation—and not in religious content. The protagonists of both poems are chiefly concerned, in Dantean terms, with the difficult transition from purgatory proper to the regained innocence of the earthly paradise, after the recognition of the anatomy of hell has been accomplished. In *The Waste Land,* of course, there is greater emphasis on communicating the recognition of hell to the reader; in *Ash-Wednesday* the central focus is on the surrender of self, the humility of prayer—on the re-creation of the meditating Ash-Wednesday communicant. The themes, symbols, and attitudes seen in this poem will dominate most of Eliot's remaining poetic production as well as *The Rock; Murder in the Cathedral;* and, to a lesser extent, the other plays.

II The Hollow Men

The persona of *The Hollow Men* defines himself in Dantean terms in sections I, II, and IV. The two epigraphs, "Mistah Kurtz—he dead" from Conrad's *Heart of Darkness* and "A penny for the Old Guy," suggest a pair of lost, violent souls that contrast with the hollow men. Kurtz in *Heart of Darkness* is called "hollow at the core," and yet his hollowness is less reprehensible than that of Eliot's hollow men. Marlowe, Conrad's narrator, describes Kurtz as "a voice"; he was a compelling speaker and writer who spouted idealisms of various sorts. Yet, when he traveled up the Congo River into the heart of Africa's darkness as an ivory trader, he succumbed to the whispering temptations of the jungle, to the primitive howling, the unsuspected appetites that Marlowe says may awake in any of us under such untrammeled conditions; and he set himself up as a god among the natives, killing at will and participating in "unspeakable" midnight rites. By such means he extorted from his territory fantastic amounts of ivory—but, as the manager (another but a less savory lost, violent soul) put it, his methods were "unsound." Finally, eaten up by jungle fever and his own insatiable burnings, Kurtz lies on a cot in the boat that is undertaking the impossible task of bringing him back to civilization; at the end, just before dying, he raises up, stares, and summarizes in a chilling, hollow voice the moral significance of what he has done: " 'The horror! The horror!' "

Eliot considered using these words as epigraph to *The Waste Land,* calling them "the most appropriate I can find, and somewhat elucidative," but he was discouraged from doing so by Ezra Pound. The epigraph of *The Hollow Men* is spoken derisively by the cabin boy who reports the end of Kurtz's supremacy to the corrupt manager and his companions. And it suggests here, as Eliot suggested elsewhere, in reference to Baudelaire, that it is better to be a lost, violent soul like Kurtz or Guy Fawkes than to be one of Dante's trimmers—those who could not make up their minds to be either good or bad, and are not even allowed into hell proper but must perpetually chase banners hither and thither "as the wind behaves" in the vestibule of hell by the banks of the tumid river Acheron.

Guy Fawkes was a key figure in the Gunpowder Plot of 1605 which, in retaliation for harsh legal measures against Catholicism, was intended to blow up the House of Lords as King James opened the session of Parliament. When the plot failed, the key figures were executed. The day is still celebrated with fireworks in England, children carrying around straw-filled effigies of Guy Fawkes and begging pennies ("A penny for the Old Guy!") with which to buy fireworks. So here is another lost, violent soul and the source of the straw-filled dummy image used in the poem as a symbol of the wastelanders with whom the persona identifies himself—as did not the protagonist of *The Waste Land.*

Three points in the Dantean scheme compose the moral ambience of *The Hollow Men:* the vestibule where the trimmers with their meaningless voices wander aimlessly; the reunion with Beatrice in the earthly paradise; and the multifoliate rose in the end of *Paradiso.* The two minor poems *Eyes that Last I Saw in Tears* and *The Wind Sprang Up at Four O'clock,* are clearly and closely associated with the parts of *The Hollow Men,* the second having originally been published with parts II and III in the 1924 *Chapbook* as *Doris's Dream Songs.*[19] What emerges from the careful consideration of all these together is a protagonist who has participated in a separation scene (something like that of Eliot's early poem *La Figlia che Piange*) and whose life is now that of a hollow man, a dead man. However, when the dawn wind springs up at four o'clock, he is dreaming of another meeting with the girl from whom he turned away. Though their parting was final for this life, he dreams still of meeting her and reestablishing a satisfactory relation. Nevertheless, when he wakes alone, trembling with tenderness, "Lips that would kiss/Form prayers to broken stone." He realizes that such a meeting in this life is impossible, and he hopes only for a meeting like that of Dante with Beatrice. Such a meeting, though, entails the derision, the sharp rebuke which Dante suffered at Beatrice's revelation. That waking from the dream to the "echo of confusing strife" comes at a moment analogous to that of Raskolnikov, who, on the banks of the river just before his awakening to a new life in the epilogue of *Crime and Punishment,* looks across to the land where the nomads roam.

The tumid river in *The Hollow Men, Eyes that Last I Saw in Tears,* and *The Wind Sprang Up at Four O'clock* becomes the Thames of Conrad's *Heart of Darkness* and of *The Waste Land,* sweating tears and oil and tar. The memories of "sunlight on a broken column" and of the "tree swinging/And voices . . . in the wind's singing" of Dante's earthly paradise are qualified by the realization that these echoes are literary and are of a reality "More distant and more solemn/Than a fading star." So the "Lips that would kiss/Form prayers to broken stone"—to the heap of broken images; the attempt is to find fulfillment in the ritual of the church at five o'clock in the morning. But this is the cactus land, so instead of the mulberry bush, *"Here we go round the prickly pear"* (they taste good, in a sparse, delicate, seedy fashion, but there are thorns). The ritual has lost its vitality. Even could the eyes be faced in dreams, even could grace restore the eyes with their rebuke and derision, this hollow man cannot bear to face the thought: "Between the idea [Dante's conception]/And the reality/. . . Falls the Shadow." Perhaps this shadow suggests the rash act that grows out of boredom, as in Conrad's story "The Shadow-Line," and also the shadow of mortality which, in Dante's progress through purgatory, continually amazes the shades who have not crossed to death's other kingdom with direct eyes. And because Eliot's protagonist is hollow, stuffed with straw, and not a man emptied of involvement in sensuous experience, he feels that, like Conrad's Marlowe, he will have nothing significant to say at his final moment—not the courage of Kurtz's "The horror! The horror!", not the bang with which Guy Fawkes intended to end his world, but only the whimper of the fading Lord's Prayer: "For Thine is/Life is/ For Thine is the."

I said earlier that *The Hollow Men* ties together the worlds of Sweeney, *The Waste Land*, Dante, *Ash-Wednesday*, and the *Four Quartets*. The title *Doris's Dream Songs* signals the relations that emerge clearly upon careful examination. It is the waste-land world of *Sweeney Agonistes* that has been arrived at after the rejection, the division from "the eyes." The Dantean framework points forward to the later works; and yet the persona, recognizing all the possibilities of the lost, violent souls and of the blest souls as well, lacks the courage to be either. He prefers to join the souls of Dante's vestibule in "Behaving as the wind behaves." Stuffed with straw like the Guy Fawkes effigies, wearing "such deliberate disguises" as his scarecrow get-up, he avoids all significant actions or decisions.

III *Ariel Poems and Others*

During the period from *The Hollow Men* (1925) to *Ash-Wednesday* (1930) were published four "Ariel poems" (the name given by the Faber firm to a series of Christmas poems): *Journey of the Magi* (1927), *A Song for Simeon* (1928), *Animula* (1929, discussed in Chapter 2), and *Marina* (1930). The first two poems have personae—comparable to Gerontion— who in each case contemplate the significance of the incarnation, the birth of Christ, which has put an end to one era and begun another, combining birth and death. *The Journey of the Magi* suggests also the epic journey of the hero myths, for after rigorous trials the hero is initiated, but then he has to return to his own world to try to make the hard adjustment of living with and of communicating his knowledge to those who have not been initiated. The Magus says,

> I had seen birth and death,
> But had thought they were different; this Birth was
> Hard and bitter agony for us, like Death, our death.
> We returned to our places, these Kingdoms,
> But no longer at ease here, in the old dispensation,
> With an alien people clutching their gods.
> I should be glad of another death.

The title character of *A Song for Simeon* is found in the biblical story of Joseph and Mary's bringing Jesus to Jerusalem to dedicate him to the Lord (Luke 2: 25-35):

> And, behold, there was a man in Jerusalem, whose name was Simeon; and the same man was just and devout, waiting for the consolation of Israel: and the Holy Ghost was upon him.
>
> And it was revealed unto him by the Holy Ghost, that he should not see death, before he had seen the Lord's Christ.
>
> And he came by the Spirit into the temple: and when the parents brought in the child Jesus, to do for him after the custom of the law,
>
> Then took he him up in his arms, and blessed God, and said,
>
> Lord, now lettest thou thy servant depart in peace, according to thy word:
>
> For mine eyes have seen thy salvation. . . .
>
> After blessing them, Simeon said to Mary,
>
> . . . Behold, this child is set for the fall and rising again of many in Israel; and for a sign which shall be spoken against;
>
> (Yea, a sword shall pierce through thy own soul also,) that the thoughts of many hearts may be revealed.

In the poem, Simeon foresees the Roman oppressions and the crucifixion; and he asks to be granted the peace of death before those things occur. Old and tired, he says: "Not for me the martyrdom, the ecstasy . . ./Not for me the ultimate vision./ Grant me thy peace." He also repeats the parenthetic "(And a sword shall pierce thy heart,/Thine also.)." Like Gerontion's, "this show" has not been made purposelessly; and yet this sign that he has seen, this unspoken Word, will be rejected by many.

In *Marina* we have one of Eliot's most appealing and best-loved poems. We need not recognize any of its echoes from either Shakespeare's *Pericles* or Seneca's *Hercules Furens* to find its tone and imagery free, open, and compelling. The reader familiar with *Pericles* will recognize that Eliot has strikingly recreated the tonality of the remarkable recognition scene in Act V of that play. The Latin epigraph from Seneca—spoken by Hercules as he comes out of a fit of madness in which, though he does not yet realize it, he has killed his children—seems to add a rather cruel qualification to the felicity of the poem. Yet, even though the song of the woodthrush may be "the deception of the thrush" (*Burnt Norton*), I would connect that deception to the earlier, unfulfilled aspirations of Pericles' youth. For we remember that in *The Waste Land* it is the hermit thrush singing in the pine trees that is longed for as a sign of the much-desired water; in *Marina*, however, the song is real, the face is real, the pulse is real; and all previous suffering fades to insignificance.

So the epigraph, on second thought, seems to form a parallel to the contrasting vices of the incestuous Antiochus and his daughter, the murderously jealous Dionyza and her compliant husband Cleon, the hired murderers, pirates, and panderers of the play, all of which Shakespeare sets against the unwavering virtues of Pericles, his daughter Marina, and his wife Thaisa. The former vices seem to be referred to in Eliot's enumeration of five of the cardinal sins. "Those who sharpen the tooth of the dog" suggests the concupiscence of a number of Shakespeare's characters. "Those who glitter with the glory of the humming-bird" suggests Antiochus' persistence in his incestuous relation, and "Those who suffer the ecstasy of the animals," the inhabitants and the patrons of the brothel from which Marina escapes unsullied. But all of these "Are become unsubstantial" by the grace of the reunions with Marina and Thaisa. "No more, you gods!" says Shakespeare's Pericles. "Your present kindness makes my past miseries sports. You shall do well that on the touching of her lips I may melt and no more be seen." This last sentence suggests the resignation of the end of *Marina*. Both the heavenly music that Shakespeare's Pericles hears, the music of the spheres, and the trembling, unbelievable surmise of fulfillment have gotten into Eliot's verse.

The boat imagery of this poem, often misinterpreted, is similar to that of Rimbaud's *Le Bateau Ivre* ("The Drunken Boat"); the boat is the speaker Pericles himself—another of Eliot's Old Man personae. Pericles' decline is referred to in the lines "Bowsprit cracked with ice and paint cracked with heat" and "The rigging weak and the canvas rotten." The "this" that he made "Between one June and another September" is Marina, his daughter. Now, though his "garboard strake leaks, [and] the seams need caulking," Marina, a new ship, will live on beyond his time. And Pericles is quite contented to "Resign my life for this life, my speech for that unspoken." Here, in perhaps the most sustained ecstasy of Eliot's poems, the deadly sins, "meaning Death," are "reduced by a wind,/A breath of pine, and the woodsong fog."

The two poems entitled *Coriolan* consider the qualities of the proper hero and statesman as contrasted with the unheroic qualities of the mob. They are contrasted further with the petty committees and commissions—with all the details of minor statesmanship which erode the heroism of the public servant and which, by forcing the compromises of which Shakespeare's Coriolanus was almost incapable, bow and dim the fierce spirit and the aggressive virtues of the statesman.

The sixth canto of Dante's *Purgatorio* seems to have provided the dicing guards, the frogs croaking in the marshes, and the theme of petty corruption in politics and civic life. The emphasis in Eliot's first *Coriolan* poem, *Triumphal March,* is on the hero as he is observed by an unidentified persona:

> There he is now, look:
> There is no interrogation in his eyes
> Or in the hands, quiet over the horse's neck,
> And the eyes watchful, waiting, perceiving, indifferent.
> O hidden under the dove's wing, hidden in the turtle's breast,
> Under the palmtree at noon, under the running water
> At the still point of the turning world. O hidden.

The significance of these eyes the persona of the poem sees, but those around him (or, just possibly, her) do not. They are occupied with such small things as the sausage that "may come in handy" later.

In *Difficulties of a Statesman*—not published separately as *Triumphal March* had been before both appeared as *Coriolan*—the time of the triumphal march is past and the details of administration are galling the hero and attenuating the calm that earlier characterized him: "O hidden under the . . . Hidden under the . . ." (Eliot's omission periods). Rather than Gerontion's "dull head among windy spaces," Coriolan says, "I a tired head among these heads." Shakespeare's Coriolanus, we remember, refused to placate "the mutable, rank-scented many"; his nature "is too noble for this world; he would not flatter Neptune for his trident." Coriolanus' fierce pride was spurred on by his mother, Volumnia, of whom he asks: "Cry what shall I cry?" But as in *The Waste Land,* this is "a broken Coriolanus," revived only "for a moment." A moment, however, can be decisive.

The five poems entitled *Five-Finger Exercises* are, like the later *Old Possum's Book of Practical Cats* (1939), delightful parodies on other poets as well as exercises in various devices and forms of verse. Nevertheless, the content of the first three of these five is serious and reflects the religious concern of the period from *The Hollow Men* to *Ash-Wednesday*. The five *Landscapes* also included in the minor poems—*New Hampshire*; *Virginia*; *Usk*; *Rannoch, by Glencoe*; and *Cape Ann*—were written during and after the year (1933) that Eliot spent in the United States after an absence of eighteen years, during which time both of his parents had died. The holocaust of World War I and the painful readjustment to its aftermath had intervened; and for about six years, Eliot had been a British subject and a member of the Anglican Church.

So the return to the home of his youth undoubtedly involved strong feelings, old and new; it seems in the poems to have introduced a type of serenity, a relaxing of the fierce striving of youth. Perhaps it is not just *Cape Ann* that is referred to in the last line of these landscapes, "The palaver is finished."

The last of the minor poems, *Lines for an Old Man,* was written for Mallarmé,[20] and certainly the potent, irritable, and dangerous quality of its persona is quite different from Eliot's others—except possibly that of *Preludes,* who says, "Wipe your hand across your mouth, and laugh;/The worlds revolve like ancient women/Gathering fuel in vacant lots." The short lines and the strong rhythms of this poem admirably match the caustic mood portrayed.

CHAPTER 6

The Second and Third Voices

ELIOT'S FIRST PROSE VOLUME, *The Sacred Wood* (1920), had included an essay on the possibility of poetic drama and another entitled "Rhetoric and Poetic Drama." And any reader of *The Criterion* from 1922 onward could not fail to note Eliot's continued editorial interest in and emphasis on theatre as well as dramatic literature. He had also written about various English dramatists, Elizabethan and other, and about Seneca and Euripides, among classical playwrights. The dramatic nature of Eliot's poetry had long testified to such interests, and hardly anyone could be surprised when in 1927 there appeared *Fragment of an Agon*, labeled then as "*From Wanna Go Home, Baby?*" In 1928 he wrote "A Dialogue on Poetic Drama"—later reprinted as "A Dialogue on Dramatic Poetry"—in which seven alphabetically designated speakers advanced various viewpoints related to the possibility of poetic drama.[1] In 1932 was added *Fragment of a Prologue*, the two poems being then entitled *Sweeney Agonistes: Fragments of an Aristophanic Melodrama*.

Though it shows the wasteland picture of Sweeney's world among the nightingales, this first overt attempt at drama was written during the same period that produced the highly Christian poem *Ash-Wednesday*. As one of the participants in Eliot's "Dialogue on Dramatic Poetry" says of Restoration drama, so criticized for its portrayal of debauchery, "It assumes orthodox Christian morality . . . It retains its respect for the divine by showing the failure of the human."[2] The title *Sweeney Agonistes* links the whole Sweeney series to the accounts of Samson both in the book of Judges and in Milton's "Samson Agonistes." Milton's portrayal of Delilah, the Philistine temptress, is echoed in Eliot's portrayal of Dusty and especially of Doris Dorrance. Samson, of course, was not only figuratively but also literally blind through lust, his plight being the direct penalty for succumbing to the beguilement of two Philistine women. Of that lust, Milton's Samson says after his blinding,

> O indignity, O blot
> To honour and religion! servile mind
> Rewarded well with servile punishment!
> The base degree to which I now am fallen,
> These rags, this grinding, is not yet so base
> As was my former servitude, ignoble,
> Unmanly, ignominious, infamous,
> True slavery; and that blindness worse than this,
> That saw not how degenerately I served.
>   (ll. 411-19)

Milton has Samson's father, Manoa, remind him that he violated "the sacred trust of silence . . . which to have kept/Tacit was in thy power." This fits well with Dante's and with Eliot's doctrine of Free Will and Temptation, of man's responsibility to guard the threshold of assent, as seen in *Animula*. Milton also shows the Philistines as morally blind when they unknowingly invite their own doom by requiring Samson to appear at their feast to the god **Dagon**:

> So fond are mortal men,
> Fallen into wrath divine,
> As their own ruin on themselves to invite,
> Insensate left, or to sense reprobate,
> And with blindness internal struck.
>   (ll. 1682-86)

Milton's Aristotelian intent to purge his audience of pity and fear is, in the final lines of "Samson Agonistes," attributed to God:

> His servants he, with new acquist
> Of true experience from this great event,
> With peace and consolation hath dismissed,
> And calm of mind, all passion spent.
>   (ll. 1755-58)

Whatever may be the relative merits of the two poets, Eliot fortunately was blessed with a surer dramatic sense than was Milton, who ends what we might label a scene by having the chorus say unexpectedly, "But had we best retire? I see a storm." This storm, though intended symbolically, reminds the reader of the many doughty heroes and dastardly villains who have "died of the fifth act." Given the stylization of the music-hall format seen in the interspersed songs of Eliot's agon, we must say that his motivations, entrances, and themes are more organic than Milton's. The rapid and powerful jazz rhythms of Eliot's fragments heighten the sense of foreboding that builds up even in the brief prologue fragment, in which the cast is introduced and the cards are read.

If the setting of *Sweeney Among the Nightingales* had seemed vague to some readers, certainly none should have been left in doubt as to that of *Sweeney Agonistes*: callers at "Miss Dorrance's *flat*" whistle below the window and call for a nose count:

>Wauchope: Hello dear
>How many's up there?
>Dusty: Nobody's up here
>How many's down there?
>Wauchope: Four of us here.
>Wait till I put the car round the corner
>We'll be right up
>Dusty: All right, come up.

Only Pereira, who pays the rent, seems unwelcome here. The moral vacuity of the characters and a strong sense of fore-boding emerge in the card-reading of Dusty and Doris which precedes the arrival of their friends, customers, guests, or whatever. Between the two fragments, Sweeney has come on the scene and is accepted by the others; but, unlike Sam Wauchope, he seems unable to be "at *home* in London." For Sweeney has seen that in their world, as on his imagined cannibal isle, there is "Nothing at all but three things/. . . Birth and copulation, and death./That's all the facts when you come to brass tacks:/Birth, and copulation, and death." Wauchope and Horsfall seem typical wasteland characters in their song:

>Tell me in what part of the wood
>Do you want to flirt with me?
>Under the breadfruit, banyan, palmleaf
>Or under the bamboo tree?
>Any old tree will do for me
>Any old wood is just as good
>Any old isle is just my style
>Any fresh egg
>Any fresh egg
>And the sound of the coral sea.

They are likely, of course, to get cooking eggs rather than any fresh egg; and Doris, for her part, says she doesn't like eggs and never has. When Sweeney introduces the idea that life and death are the same—that birth and death, as seen in *A Song for Simeon* and *The Journey of the Magi,* are hard to distinguish—Doris, who drew the coffin (the two of spades), exclaims, "Oh Mr. Sweeney, please dont talk/. . . I dont care for such conversation/A woman runs a terrible risk." Sweeney alone of the characters seems to have some idea of the nature of the terrain in which they appear; in answer to their wrong questions, he repeats, ". . . that dont apply/But I've gotta use words when I talk to you," and again, "But if you understand or if you dont/That's nothing to me and nothing to you . . ."

These fragments were enough to reveal a remarkable gift of speech and pacing, of incision and intensity in the writing of drama. Moreover, the compelling jazz rhythms, the moral bankruptcy of the setting and situation, and the personal *angst* of the characters involved are almost overwhelming. In a sense, this clarity and this concision are probably the cause as well as the result of the work's being unfinished: what Eliot set out to do in the play seems to have been accomplished, and (unlike the makers of such midcentury movies as *La Dolce Vita*) Eliot knew when to quit. In sketching in his characters and setting, he evoked the psychic or moral assessment, the purgation of pity and fear, at which the whole was aimed. The stumbling block to completion was probably the discovery that dramatic form requires the writer to focus on an action, not just a mood. Something else, therefore, would have to be attempted in the next play. So if the "meaning" of *Sweeney Agonistes* is quite similar to that of *Sweeney Among the Nightingales,* its form identifies the point from which each of Eliot's plays was to represent another successive step and development in dramatic understanding and technique.

I The Rock

Eliot's interest in poetic drama was given added stimulation by the commission to write the words to the religious pageant-play *The Rock* (1934). Frankly didactic, it was written "on behalf of the Forty-Five Churches Fund of the Diocese of London." The pageant explores on several levels the meaning of the building of a church. It crosses the boundaries of time and makes co-existent on the stage the Saxon king and his subjects as they hear of the Christian faith from the monk Mellitus, first Bishop of London; Rahere, a monk of King Henry's time who was also a London church-builder; the Israelites who rebuilt Jerusalem; the martyrs of the Danish invasion; Blomfield, a Bishop of London who built two hundred churches; some departing crusaders; and the twentieth-century workers who also are laboring against many difficulties to build a London church.

All of these serve to show that in no time has the work of the church been easy or unopposed. The Rock, a seer-like figure whose first entrance borrows from that of Tiresias in Sophocles' *Oedipus Rex*, stands on a pinnacle watching the building of the church and says,

> I have known two worlds, I have known two worlds of death.
>
> . . . .
>
> Does the spring change, does the bird's wing change, does the
>   fly alter
> Its purpose since the amber-time, the old time?
> There shall be always the Church and the World
> And the Heart of Man
> Shivering and fluttering between them, choosing and chosen,
> Valiant, ignoble, dark and full of light
> Swinging between Hell Gate and Heaven Gate.
> And the Gates of Hell shall not prevail.
> Darkness now, then
> Light.
>
> Light.[3]

The book of words that Eliot wrote conformed to a committee-written scenario, and the poet was careful to point out that, except for one scene and the choruses, he was responsible for only the words, not the plot, and that much of the whole had been rewritten with the expert advice of E. Martin Browne (who directed not only *The Rock* but also several of Eliot's later and more successful plays). Despite that disclaimer and the fact that only the choruses (entirely his own work) are reprinted in *The Complete Poems and Plays, 1909-1950, The Rock* is extremely interesting and "somewhat elucidative" in tying together and explicitly stating themes that appear both in the previous poetry and in the shortly to appear *Murder in the Cathedral*. In its speech patterns and rhythms *The Rock* also looked forward to the plays to come, and its use of the chorus foreshadowed that which in *Murder in the Cathedral* was to impress at least one critic as "the greatest choral poetry yet written in English."⁴ A sample from Chorus VII may illustrate:

> Then came, at a predetermined moment, a moment in time and of time,
> A moment not out of time, but in time, in what we call history; transecting, bisecting the world of time, a moment in time but not like a moment of time,
> A moment in time but time was made through that moment: for without the meaning there is no time, and that moment of time gave the meaning.
> Then it seemed as if men must proceed from light to light, in the light of the Word,
>
> . . . .
>
> But it seems that something has happened that has never happened before: though we know not just when, or why, or how, or where.
> Men have left God not for other gods, they say, but for no god . . .
>
> . . . .
>
> The Church disowned, the tower overthrown, the bells upturned, what have we to do
> But stand with empty hands and palms turned upwards
> In an age which advances progressively backwards?⁵

The audience is reminded by this pageant-play, as later by *Murder in the Cathedral,* of the continual necessity to do the work of the church in the face of adversity: "Remembering the words of Nehemiah the Prophet: 'The trowel in hand, and the gun rather loose in the holster.' "⁶ In context, this line effectively mediates between history or tradition and the present; such mediation was to remain a frequent and successful technique in all of Eliot's future plays.

Both *Sweeney Agonistes* and *The Rock* were affected by the music-hall revue, which Eliot felt was perhaps the appropriate form for modern poetic drama. In 1920 he wrote, "Possibly the majority of attempts to confect a poetic drama have begun at the wrong end; they have aimed at the small public which wants 'poetry.' . . . The Elizabethan drama was aimed at a public which wanted *entertainment* of a crude sort, but would *stand* a good deal of poetry; our problem should be to take a form of entertainment, and subject it to the process which would leave it a form of art. Perhaps the music-hall comedian is the best material."[7]

In a later essay about writing poetry, Eliot distinguishes among the poet's three "voices": first, "the voice of the poet talking to himself—or to nobody"; second, "the voice of the poet addressing an audience"; and third, "the voice of the poet when he attempts to create a dramatic character speaking in verse; when he is saying, not what he would say in his own person, but only what he can say within the limits of one imaginary character addressing another imaginary character."[8] He says that not until 1938, after the completion of both *The Rock* and *Murder in the Cathedral*, did that third voice begin "to force itself upon [his] ear."

What he did learn from *The Rock* chiefly concerned the choruses: in them, he says, "it was the second voice, that of myself addressing—indeed haranguing—an audience, that was most distinctly audible. Apart from the obvious fact that writing to order is not the same thing as writing to please oneself, I learnt only that verse to be spoken by a choir should be different from verse to be spoken by one person; and that the more voices you have in your choir, the simpler and more direct the vocabulary, the syntax, and the content of your lines must be. This chorus of *The Rock* was not a dramatic voice; though many lines were distributed, the personages were unindividuated. Its members were speaking *for me*, not uttering words that really represented any supposed character of their own."[9] That last criticism, though convincing, does not keep the choruses from *The Rock* from being very good poetry nor the whole work from achieving its intended effects. I would argue that *The Rock* is a much more effective piece of theatre than its brief dismissal by most critics and by Eliot himself might suggest; Eliot's criticism that the chorus was his own voice, not an individualized identity satisfactorily integrated into the dramatic structure, is valid but not damning. It does, however, help to explain the greater success of the choruses in the next two plays.

II Murder in the Cathedral

With the 1935 Canterbury Festival performance of *Murder in the Cathedral*[10] in the Chapter House where the murder had taken place in 1170, Eliot was revealed as an assured and powerful dramatic poet. Such an emphatic success was perhaps not wholly predictable, nor was the precise nature of the subject matter of this play: martyrdom. As Leonard Unger says, "The alienation of Prufrock *et al* is remodeled into the alienation of the saint; yet the predicament of Prufrock would not become the predicament of Becket—if it had not."[11]

The Rock seems the link which connects this great play to Eliot's earlier work, and the difference in the conditions under which the two were written probably explains the differences in merit between the two. In *Murder in the Cathedral,* though he was again writing on commission for the church, Eliot was the sole author; for not just the book of words but the total conception was his. This situation allowed him to produce a much tighter artistic unity, one in which no element is extraneous nor merely repetitive. Probably the author found his subject while working on *The Rock,* and certainly he profited greatly by the experience of working on the actual productions of both works with E. Martin Browne. From this experience came a pattern that was to produce great differences among his future plays: From each of his plays he was to draw specific lessons and apply them to the next; in each he attempted something significantly different from the last. To the practicing dramatic poet, this was dictated by a logic of necessity, a necessity not inevitably apparent to one only interested in reading or in seeing the plays. As D. E. Jones points out, in the early plays Eliot intentionally kept the audience aware that they were listening to poetry. Each of the later plays was to be written at a lower and lower level of poetic intensity, until the author could say of *The Cocktail Party* that it was questionable whether it contained any real poetry at all—an obvious exaggeration.

The fact that *Murder in the Cathedral* was to be performed before an officially Christian audience in a cathedral and as part of a Christian festival had much to do with both the choice of subject and the treatment given it. These factors made it plausible, for instance, to follow the classical unities of place and action rather closely; and they also made it natural to use a sermon as interlude. They also importantly influenced the character and the use of the chorus, and they suggested the direct involvement of the audience, so effectively achieved through the use of the Knights' speeches, the sermon, and the choruses.

Like *Burnt Norton* (1936) this play is concerned with the "enchainment of past and future/Woven in the weakness of the changing body" and with the still point of the turning world where past and future are gathered. Both are concerned with "abstention from movement; while the world moves/In appetency, on its metalled ways/Of time past and time future." But in the play, all this was channelled through the one vividly individualized character, Thomas. The play goes behind the mere historical facts of his martyrdom to show us the inner experience, its inner meaning. It makes of Thomas, though he is still a particular individual, a symbol of the meaning of all martyrdoms, of the life of the church in its struggle against the world, and a symbol also of the meaning embodied in the particular consecrated place that is Canterbury Cathedral. It makes the audience consider these questions: "What *are* we, what *should* we be, and what *can* we be?" Like *The Rock*, it reminds the spectators that their struggles and their responsibilities echo those of the church in all times. It further reminds them that only by getting beyond involvement with the particular occurrence can one discover the meaning that gives peace and fulness to an experience.

The plot of *Murder in the Cathedral* may be summarized as follows: The chorus of women of Canterbury and the three priests receive word that Thomas, their archbishop, is about to return after seven years in exile. They express doubts and forebodings as to what shall follow, calling his reconciliation with the King uncertain. As the women lament his return, which may upset their small routines, and the priests urge them to welcome the archbishop, Thomas himself enters. He makes it clear that his return was opposed and awaited by many enemies, and that they will soon descend on him; and adds, "Meanwhile the substance of our first act/Will be shadows, and the strife with shadows," just as the First Tempter enters. This figure from the past tempts him with pleasures of the past, to which Thomas replies:

> Men learn little from others' experience.
> But in the life of one man, never
> The same time returns. Sever
> The cord, shed the scale. Only
> The fool, fixed in his folly, may think
> He can turn the wheel on which he turns.

The First Tempter leaves and the Second Tempter enters to offer the chancellorship which Thomas once held, if only he will give up his archbishopric. "No!" says Thomas,

> . . . shall I, who keep the keys
> Of heaven and hell, supreme alone in England,
> Who bind and loose, with power from the Pope,
> Descend to a punier power?

and the Second Tempter leaves. The Third Tempter comes to offer "a happy coalition of intelligent interests," those of Thomas and those of the barons against the King. He is also dismissed and an unexpected Fourth Tempter appears. His temptation is that Thomas shall become a martyr for the wrong motives—his own eternal glory and pride. Recognizing his own desires in this, Thomas almost despairs: "Is there no way, in my soul's sickness,/Does not lead to damnation in pride?" After the Tempters, Priests, and Chorus have echoed the welter of impulses, fears, and forebodings implicit in the situation, the Chorus implores, "save yourself that we may be saved," and Thomas sees his way clear. He has vanquished this last and greatest of the Tempters, and he will now avoid doing the right deed, martyrdom, for the wrong reason, pride. Thomas' comedy is now complete, and the Interlude and Act II serve to complete those of the Chorus, Thomas' Canterbury sermon audience, and the twentieth-century audience of Eliot's play.

The Interlude between Part I and Part II is a Christmas sermon on the nature of the peace heralded at Christ's birth and of the martyrdom that falls the lot of some of those who achieve that mysterious peace: "A martyrdom is never the design of man; for the true martyr is he who has become the instrument of God, who has lost his will in the will of God, not lost it but found it, for he has found freedom in submission to God. The martyr no longer desires anything for himself, not even the glory of martyrdom."

In Part II the Chorus signifies its acceptance of its part in Thomas' martyrdom, and then the four knights who will murder him make their first appearance. They make their demands and accusations and almost attack Thomas, but they leave when the priests and attendants intervene. Several weeks later (December 29, 1170) they return and kill Thomas, who accepts his death willingly in spite of his priests' attempts to hide him.

The knights then address the audience and attempt to explain away their guilt and to implicate the audience in it. They plead their disinterestedness and sacrifice, Thomas' reversal of his policies after the king had caused him to be made archbishop, and the necessity of protecting the State against the pretensions of the church. Finally the Fourth Knight, Richard Brito, urges that Thomas had determined to die a martyr and is really guilty of "Suicide while of Unsound Mind."

The Chorus, however, and the priests, reject the knights' reasoning and dismiss them to their empty fate, accepting and rejoicing in the significance of Thomas' martyrdom, which renews the sanctity of their time and place and delineates the contrast between the life of the world and the life of the church, between which hovers the soul of man.

Murder in the Cathedral might be called the most obviously successful of Eliot's plays. The consistent purpose of the play is to share revitalization of a whole world-view with the audience. As already suggested, the audience is irresistibly drawn into the action and made to feel co-responsible for it. What Eliot shares with his audience is not philosophy nor theology in the abstract, but the emotional and muscular feel of belief in a world-view that has divine incarnation and Christian martyrdom as its most significant and perpetual truths, a world-view that emphasizes the dichotomy of the two lives of the world and the church, between which man's soul is balanced. The play emphasizes the necessity of perpetually renewing the awareness of the mysteries which comprise the links between the two lives.

The choruses in this play represent an advance over those of *The Rock*, for the lines spoken are matched to the general character of the women of Canterbury, but the members of the chorus are not distinguished one from another. When Eliot collaborated with George Hoellering in making a film of *Murder in the Cathedral*, lines of the chorus were assigned to individual women seen in the film at their daily tasks as they spoke. (Eliot and Hoellering in the prefaces to their 1952 book *The Film of Murder in the Cathedral*[12] provocatively discuss the problems of adaptation from stage to film.) There is some individualization of the priests in the play, but there is more between the knights and between the tempters who accost Thomas. The knights and tempters link the levels of the play's meanings. Though quite plausible on the literal level, both groups step back and forth between levels of meaning. The tempters seem even more real on the psychological plane, and indeed in the film the Fourth Tempter was represented only by a voice (that of the poet himself) that is listened to and challenged by Thomas as he wrestles with wrong motives and finally vanquishes them.

Parts I and II of the play are separated by an interlude which is Thomas' Christmas sermon on the mysteries of incarnation and martyrdom, paradoxically evoking joy and grief simultaneously. As the sermon continues, Thomas' congregation expands to include the modern audience and to prepare them, as it did the humble folk of Thomas' Canterbury, to understand the meaning of his death:

> A martyrdom is never the design of man; for the true martyr is he who has become the instrument of God, who has lost his will in the will of God, not lost it but found it, for he has found freedom in submission to God. The martyr no longer desires anything for himself, not even the glory of martyrdom.
> . . . I have spoken to you today, dear children of God, of the martyrs of the past, asking you to remember especially our martyr of Canterbury, the blessed Archbishop Elphege; because it is fitting, on Christ's birthday, to remember what is that Peace which He brought; and because, dear children, I do not think I shall ever preach to you again; and because it is possible that in a short time you may have yet another martyr, and that one perhaps not the last. I would have you keep in your hearts these words that I say, and think of them at another time.

For the film, Eliot wrote an earlier opening scene showing the struggle between Thomas and King Henry II. Though Eliot is undoubtedly correct in his suggestion that this scene should not be played on the stage, it seems to me an effective addition to the reading of the play. (Eliot's preface to the film version might well be expanded to include this third—and bastard?—art form, the reading of a play.)

Through the strong rhythms and imagery of his language, especially in the choruses, Eliot recreates for the reader or listener the feeling of significant involvement in the moral and religious scheme implied. We can imagine that this was true to a remarkable degree for the audience at the original performances. The sermon which forms the interlude between Parts I and II is Thomas' attempt to involve his own congregation in the same awareness; and, though the knights in Part II tempt the audience somewhat as Thomas was tempted by the tempters and with considerable show of logic (only part of it specious), the audience may be counted on to agree at the end with the attitudes of the chorus and of the third priest, who condemns the knights:

> Go, weak sad men, lost erring souls, homeless in earth or heaven.
> Go where the sunset reddens the last grey rock
> Of Brittany, or the Gates of Hercules.
> . . . .
>
> Or sit and bite your nails in Aquitaine.
> In the small circle of pain within the skull
> You still shall tramp and tread one endless round
> Of thought, to justify your actions to yourselves,
> Weaving a fiction which unravels as you weave,
> Pacing forever in the hell of make-believe
> Which never is belief: this is your fate on earth
> And we must think no further of you. . . .

The knights seem hardly lost violent souls, but only the hollow men of the unreal city, the trimmers of Dante's vestibule; the cathedral before which the play is set seems to have become before the eyes of the audience holy ground from which the sanctity shall not depart "though armies trample over it, though sightseers come with guide-books looking over it."

That the play should have been an overwhelming success at the Canterbury Festival with a Christian audience is not at all surprising; but a greater testimony to its dramatic and poetic virtues is the success that it achieved in commercial and educational theatres throughout the world. But as Eliot and a number of commentators have said, it was hardly a repeatable success; and much of what fused together so vividly in this drama had necessarily to be abandoned in the next one—a play not less impressive, though less acclaimed. *The Family Reunion,* though it lacks the tight unity of *Murder in the Cathedral,* also expands the potentialities of the English dramatic tradition. But it does so in somewhat different directions.

III   The Family Reunion

In *The Family Reunion* (1939) Eliot explored, as is indicated in the title and the use of the Eumenides, the meaning of the curse that was so integral a part of the great Greek tragedies— but a part that the modern audience is likely to find puzzling and either irrelevant or anachronistic. The effect of *The Family*

Reunion is to recreate the relevance, to make the curse seem meaningful in twentieth-century terms. The play even goes a long way toward reconciling and tempering the seeming injustice of the biblical curse that the sins of the father shall be visited on the sons to the third and fourth generations. This is accomplished by portraying the emotional inevitability of the recurrent psychic pattern of those violations against the proper familial and reproductive cycles that underlie the curses on the houses of Atreus, Thyestes, and Harry Lord Monchensey.

The Family Reunion is set in Wishwood, the country house of the Monchenseys. For the first time in eight years, they are having a family reunion. Three of them, Arthur, John, and Harry, have not yet arrived. The Chorus is composed, from time to time, of Ivy, Violet, Gerald, and Charles, sisters and brothers-in-law of Amy, Dowager Lady Monchensey. Agatha, another sister, shows herself almost from the start to be more perceptive and less blinded by petty immediacies than the rest. Mary, the daughter of a cousin and the youngest member of the family present, seems also freer of the misconceptions and myopia of the others.

Before Harry arrives, it is made clear that he married eight years ago against the wishes of the family and has not been back since. His wife has died about a year previously, the conditions of her disappearance from shipdeck in a storm not being very clear. At Harry's appearance, it is clear that all is not well. He believes that he murdered his wife, and now for the first time he sees the Furies that have pursued him since her death. The family is convinced that he is suffering delusions of guilt.

Agatha and Mary understand more of their and Harry's problems than he does, and for a moment Mary has given Harry again the hope that he thought was forever gone, but the reappearance of the Furies breaks their rapport. As the play progresses, the nature of Harry's malady and of the significance of the spectres appearing to him becomes clearer through his discussions with Dr. Warburton, the family physician, and especially with Agatha. She tells him of her affair with his father which is the origin of the curse he will now have to expiate, and, as he comes to understand, he accepts the spectres —says he will seek, rather than flee, them from now on. He prepares to leave. Not only Harry, but also Agatha, Mary, and his mother Amy have reached the point at which illusions are falling away and new starts must be made. Amy, though, is too old and tired; with understanding comes death. She leaves behind Agatha and Mary, wandering in "the neutral territory/ Between two worlds"—that into which Harry has crossed and that in which the rest of the family continues unaware of the other.

To some extent, Eliot's play is based on Aeschylus' *Oresteia* trilogy (*Agamemnon, The Choëphoroe, The Eumenides*), the only surviving complete trilogy from the golden age of Athenian tragedy. Eliot did not, however, follow closely or slavishly the patterns of Aeschylus. Harry Lord Monchensey is comparable to Orestes, but his expiation of the curse through suffering has begun before the death of his mother. Indeed, we could hardly call Harry's decision to leave Wishwood a matricide in spite of Dr. Warburton's previous warning that any shock might cause Amy's immediate death (as Harry's departure does). In fact, Harry, Agatha, and Mary believe that his leaving is absolutely essential to the expiation of the family curse. And Downing, Harry's chauffeur (Krishna, the charioteer?) and the first person able to see the Eumenides, had foreseen the necessity of their leaving, just as he foresees that Harry will not need him or any-one else much longer.

It remains doubtful whether Harry has actually committed any murder. "Perhaps," he says, "my life has only been a dream/ Dreamt through me by the minds of others." And of his wife's drowning, he adds, "Perhaps/I only dreamt I pushed her." Agatha replies, "So I had supposed." Perhaps he is personally guilty only of the desire to get rid of her, just as his father was guilty only of the desire to murder Amy. And yet it is the desire, the intent, the psychic posture involved in the curse, to which the Furies or the Eumenides are related. The act itself, as Harry points out, is the accident of a moment, seeming almost unrelated to the continuing identity of the actor:

> It is really harder to believe in murder
> Than to believe in cancer. Cancer is here:
> The lump, the dull pain, the occasional sickness:
> Murder a reversal of sleep and waking.
> Murder was there. Your ordinary murderer
> Regards himself as an innocent victim.*
> To himself he is still what he used to be
> Or what he would be. He cannot realize
> That everything is irrevocable,
> The past unredeemable.
> *[cf. Raskolnikov in *Crime and Punishment*]

But whether or not he *indulged* the impulse, the murderer can escape it only through the slow purgational movement of a psychic reorientation whose magnitude is measured by the fact of the Eumenides' appearing; and a single lifetime is likely to be too short to make such a transition, human nature and nurture being what they are. Only when Athena steps in is Orestes' expiation fulfilled, and only with the help of Mary and Agatha is Harry brought to understand not only the nature of the curse but also the nature and use of the Eumenides, whom he will henceforth hunt rather than flee ("Then dived he back back into the fire . . .").

At the beginning of the play, Harry thinks of himself as alone with his problems and as solely capable of understanding and facing them. He feels that all his life has been determined by his mother Amy and that he has been prevented from living for himself, as he now insists on doing. Later, when Agatha tells him about his father and her affair with him, he sees himself as reunited to the family and as one who has fulfilled a pattern, a curse on the whole family, fulfilled earlier by his father—perhaps not for the first time. In realizing this Harry understands that the Furies which plague him are the necessary agents of expiation and that only by accepting the natures of himself and his family can he successfully escape from what he has been, can he "unknot the knot," "uncross the cross," "make straight the crooked," and end the curse.

The other characters of the play (who see only one world) try, as Harry tells them, "to think of each thing separately/ Making small things important, so that everything/May be unimportant." Later they say in chorus, "We have suffered far more than a personal loss—/We have lost our way in the dark." Harry's repeated insistence that none of them can understand his problem, his decision, or his language leads Agatha to protest that, whatever he has learned, he must remember that there is always more; and Mary says that she thinks she could understand, but he would have to be patient.

As in *Murder in the Cathedral*, Eliot in *The Family Reunion* has the members of the chorus vitally involved in the plot. They are Harry's aunts Ivy and Violet and his uncles Gerald and Charles. Their concerted speeches, in which they express their unenlightened condition and the emotions that go along with it, are punctuated by individual lines in which they characterize themselves or one another. The sentiments expressed are usually of foreboding and futility. In their final speech, the "We have lost our way in the dark" line is completed after individual lines by "But we must adjust ourselves to the moment: we must do the right thing." The final incantation on the nature of a curse and of redemption from it is chanted not by the Chorus but by Agatha and Mary. Its concluding lines emphasize what Agatha has already suggested: that it is not only the living but also the dead for whom the curse is expiated; that Harry, as she told him earlier, may be "the consciousness of your unhappy family,/Its bird sent flying through the purgatorial flame." In the same speech she told him that all of them have written "not a story of detection,/Of crime and punishment, but of sin and expiation." (This, of course, is what Dostoyevsky really wrote too in his *Crime and Punishment*; any other reading must ignore the role of Porfiry Petrovitch, the Epilogue, and the underlying structural principle of the novel and its unity.) She tells him that though he may not yet have known "what sin/You shall expiate, or whose, or why, . . . the knowledge of it must precede the expiation."

At the end of the play we are left in the dark as to exactly what form Harry's expiation will take after he leaves; and yet it does not matter. As Dostoyevsky says in the Epilogue to his *Crime and Punishment,* "But that is the beginning of a new story—the story of the gradual renewal of a man, the story of his gradual regeneration, of his passing from one world into another, of his initiation into a new unknown life. That might be the subject of a new story, but our present story is ended."[13]

And in *The Cocktail Party,* Eliot's next play, Sir Henry Harcourt-Reilly makes it clear that the precise manner of the death of Celia Coplestone, who is in some ways comparable to Harry, did not matter. It is to emphasize this point that Eliot has Lavinia watch Sir Henry's face as Alex describes Celia's martyrdom and note that he seems to experience satisfaction in the manner of her death. When she questions him about his apparent satisfaction, he replies that on first meeting Celia he had intuitively seen the image "Of a Celia Coplestone whose face showed the astonishment/Of the first five minutes after a violent death." Knowing that violent death was her destiny, he could only help her choose the way of life that would prepare her for it properly. And he concludes, ". . . if that is not a happy death, what death is happy?"

There are significant parallels between Reilly's description of the image that he saw and Eliot's use of the Eumenides in *The Family Reunion.* Reilly quotes Shelley on the Magus Zoroaster, who

> Met his own image walking in the garden.
> That apparition, sole of men, he saw.
> For know there are two worlds of life and death:
> One that which thou beholdest; but the other
> Is underneath the grave, where do inhabit
> The shadows of all forms that think and live
> Till death unite them and they part no more.

This passage suggests the "tougher selves" of which Edward speaks in *The Cocktail Party* and also the psyches of Harry and Agatha in *The Family Reunion,* which they are painfully trying to discover. The Eumenides, however, are supra-personal, representing the moral forces that are unbalanced by the wrong tendencies involved in the curse on Harry's house, the sin which must be expiated and the forces demanding its expiation before balance can be restored. And the "loop in time" which has brought Harry back face to face with that issue has also placed him in a position to expiate the curse and to free the family of it just as Orestes was able, finally, to free his.

As C. L. Barber has pointed out, Eliot in this play has largely eschewed Christian symbols: "The public at large beat a path, it is true, to *Murder in the Cathedral.* But most of them went as sightseers, ready to forget their own standards when these were burlesqued in the murderers' Erastian apologies, but in a spirit which regarded as historical not only the events, but also the Christian values and standards of the play. In *The Family Reunion* Eliot has deliberately made impossible any such facile acceptance of the reality of the supernatural. He has sought to confront the modern world with the necessity of redemption at its starkest, without benefit of clergy."[14]

The use of the Eumenides has called forth more criticism, perhaps, than any other aspect of the play. For the modern audience such a device is likely to be jarring, and Eliot has said that it is very difficult to stage properly the scenes in which they appear. Nevertheless, they seem to fit well with the stylization of the trancelike speeches of Harry, Agatha, and the chorus; with the explicit shifts in levels of meaning; and with the anti-literal tone that recurrently emerges—elements not necessarily derived from Greek tragedy. They effectively stop any tendency of the audience to interpret the play realistically at the literal level or to ignore the degree of reality attached in the play to psychic and moral—religious—life. It even seems to me that the audience need supply no knowledge of the Greek use of the Eumenides in order to grasp their significance in this play. The play in its own terms justifies their use.

Though it must be admitted that the play has its deficiencies, and that much of it is likely to be missed in a first viewing by an auditor unfamiliar with the themes that Eliot characteristically handles and with the Dantean frame of reference, *The Family Reunion* represents no small achievement; it makes not only understandable but also relevant to twentieth-century life the Greeks' use of the family curse and its role in the individual's quest for identity and felicity. The play will certainly appeal to a more limited audience than *Murder in the Cathedral* or *The Cocktail Party*, but for those familiar with the whole body of Eliot's works, it is a play likely to be esteemed more and more on each reading. Like *Crime and Punishment*, its relevance is greatest for the guilty—but no stones were cast after Christ's injunction "Let him who is without sin among you cast the first stone."

CHAPTER 7

Where Every Word Is at Home

ELIOT'S ACKNOWLEDGED poetic masterpiece has proved to be his last major, nondramatic poetry. It is really four great poems which, taken together, comprise one masterwork of philosophical poetry: the *Four Quartets*. The first of these, *Burnt Norton* (1936), as already noted, was written during the period following *The Rock* and *Murder in the Cathedral*. Eliot has indicated that some of its parts were originally intended for *Murder in the Cathedral*. The second quartet, *East Coker*, was published on Good Friday of 1940, the year following the appearance of *The Family Reunion* and the demise of the *Criterion*. The third, *The Dry Salvages*, was written in 1941, and *Little Gidding* first appeared in 1942 when all four were published under the title *Four Quartets*.

Long before 1948, when Eliot received the Nobel Prize for Literature, *Four Quartets* had been hailed by critics as the crowning achievement of a distinguished poetic career; and *Little Gidding*, the fourth, is so peculiarly conclusive that it would be hard to imagine what the poet could yet write in the poetic veins and modes that have been explored throughout the entire body of his poetry and that culminated in the *Quartets*.[1]

I Burnt Norton

The epigraphs to *Burnt Norton* are two fragments from Heraclitus; the first in translation reads "But though the Word [Logos] is common, the many live as though they had a wisdom of their own"; the second: "The road up and the road down are one and the same." These, unlike most of Eliot's earlier epigraphs, point to the central themes not only of *Burnt Norton* but of all four quartets: the doctrine of the Logos, the Word, the Word without a word, in the world and for the world—the capitalized *Word* which fuses into the uncapitalized *word* of the poet that, if right, has its own tongue of fire; these are themes central to the *Four Quartets*.

These poems, like those most admired by Eliot—Lucretius' *On the Nature of Things* (*De rerum natura*), Dante's *Divine Comedy,* and the *Bhagavad-Gita*—are philosophical poems; and their main theme is one emphasized in Eliot's writings from 1917 onwards, and it is also a perception structurally implicit in Dante's *Comedy*: the necessity of detaching oneself from total involvement in the transient life of the senses and of seeing behind the accidents of time the whole panorama of simultaneous moral order; the need to see in the happenings of one's own life and "In the agony of others, nearly experienced, /Involving ourselves" and in the myths, tales, and literature of our culture—classical, biblical, and modern—the emotional, psychic, and religious truths reflected in the postures of the souls involved in those experiences and accounts. As Eliot wrote in 1929, "The *Divine Comedy* is a complete scale of the *depths* and *heights* of human emotion; . . . the *Purgatorio* and *Paradiso* are to be read as extensions of the ordinarily very limited human range. Every degree of humanity, from lowest to highest, has, moreover, an intimate relation to the next above and below, and all fit together according to the logic of sensibility."[2]

The Word, or Logos, or Love, stands for the organizing principle of the total scheme that is grasped at rare moments of illumination or that is seen steadily by the saint. And in *Four Quartets,* as throughout Eliot's poetry, the task of grasping the whole scheme is closely related to the poet's task of understanding, finding words for, and communicating his relation to and his role in the scheme. As with Dante, the proper "making" of the poem is a form of right action and a part of the religious duty of the poet. Hence we see in the fifth section of each of the quartets some study of those problems of the poet; and we see throughout the quartets the continual recurrence of concern with the word, capitalized or uncapitalized. Hence also the concern with the incarnation, the "impossible union" of the divine and earthly spheres; with the simultaneous expanse of "the sea" which makes up the whole scheme, and "the river" of man's experience in time, so that incarnation and Christ become symbols of the moment of illumination and of the life of the saint which burns in every moment.

The chief "idea" of Section I of *Burnt Norton* is contained in the repeated couplet that ends that section: "What might have been and what has been/Point to one end, which is always present." This couplet first occurs after a more conventional consideration of attitudes towards past, present, and future. Though in Dante's purgatory and in *Ash-Wednesday* it is conceivable that one can "Redeem the time, redeem the dream" and "Redeem /The unread vision in the higher dream," in *Burnt Norton* we are told that "if all time is eternally present/All time is unredeemable." The title of the poem and its setting are taken from "an uninhabited mansion, erected on the site of an earlier house two hundred years burnt" in the Cotswolds which Eliot visited in the summer of 1934.[3] On the literal level, the visitor seems to look around the house, to disturb the dust on a bowl of rose leaves, and then to walk out into the formal rose garden and to the empty pool. This deserted garden echoes Swinburne's "The Forsaken Garden" and the dead lovers there evoked; but the blurring in *Burnt Norton*'s opening lines of distinctions between what might have been and what has been make it unnecessary to worry whether the poem's speaker visited the garden with an actual or potential lover or whether that companion too was something that might have been. At any rate this garden reminds the speaker of the lovers pondered by Swinburne's protagonist, who says,

> If a step should sound or a word be spoken,
> Would a ghost not rise at the strange guest's hand?
>
> . . . .
>
> Not a flower to be pressed of the foot that falls not;
> As the heart of a dead man the seedplots are dry;
> From the thicket of thorns whence the nightingale calls not,
> Could she call, there were never a rose to reply.
>
> . . . .
>
> Here there was laughing of old, there was weeping,
> Haply, of lovers none ever will know,
> Whose eyes went seaward a hundred sleeping
> Years ago.
> Heart handfast in heart as they stood, "Look thither,"
> Did he whisper? "look forth from the flowers to the sea;
> For the foam-flowers endure when the rose-blossoms wither,
> And men that love lightly may die—but we?"[4]

Perhaps these echoes inhabit the garden of *Burnt Norton* and are referred to as "they." The garden and the "first gate" that leads to it are referred to again in *The Family Reunion*: Agatha says to Harry (Part Two, Scene Two), "I only looked through the little door/When the sun was shining on the rose-garden:/ And heard in the distance tiny voices/And then a black raven flew over./And then I was only my own feet walking/Away, down a concrete corridor/In a dead air." After each of them tells of the torment that followed a moment of ecstasy and continued until they found release from their prisons, Harry says, "I was not there, you were not there, only our phantasms/ And what did not happen is as true as what did happen,/O my dear, and you walked through the little door/And I ran to meet you in the rose-garden."

The similarity to the imagery of *Burnt Norton*, Part I, is striking; and both throw light on the meaning of parts I and V of *The Waste Land*. Hugh Kenner, who pointed out the derivation of the five-part structure of the quartets from that of *The Waste Land* and *Ash-Wednesday*, showed convincing parallels in each case; and Kristian Smidt has shown significant parallels between *Burnt Norton* and parts IV and V of *Ash-Wednesday*. It is the *Waste Land* parallel, though, that is relevant to *Burnt Norton*; in the "hyacinth girl" episode of the earlier poem the phrase "heart of light" follows the sexual experience that so strongly echoes *Tristan und Isolde*: "—Yet when we came back, late, from the Hyacinth garden,/Your arms full, and your hair wet, I could not/Speak, and my eyes failed, I was neither/Living nor dead, and I knew nothing,/ Looking into the heart of light, the silence."

Now, in *Burnt Norton*, as the lovers look down into the drained concrete pool, suddenly "the pool was filled with water out of sunlight,/And the lotos rose, quietly, quietly,/The surface glittered out of heart of light,/And they were behind us, reflected in the pool./Then a cloud passed, and the pool was empty." The moment of extreme felicity results in *The Waste Land* from the hyacinth-garden embrace, and in *Burnt Norton* it probably derives from the imagined experience of "what might have been" or of "what was" with earlier and other lovers. It is a moment of illumination in which moral and psychic truth may be grasped—in which the distinctions between past, present, and future are erased and in which all the implications of various experiences are simultaneously present.

Here, at a moment in time, time has been conquered, but such perceptions cannot be sustained by humankind, and the voice of the bird distracts to other thoughts. Yet this perception of the nature of love, whether based on past experience in time or speculation on what might have been, points to one end: the Love, or Logos, or Word that orders the entire universe and moves the individual soul to move and act, the motive which is always present. In stirring these memories and the reader's speculations about such matters, the words of the speaker echo thus in our minds, disturbing the dust on a bowl of rose leaves—on what is left of the earlier rose-garden experience. And the bird's call is "the deception of the thrush" that leads us back to those experiences rather than to the meaning. Yet even out of these things can grow the moment of illumination, the brief recognition of the Logos.

Part II of *Burnt Norton* is a many-faceted consideration of the moment of illumination, the moment in and out of time in which the pattern is grasped, as will be further considered in the fifth section of the poem. This is the moment in the rose-garden;[5] the moment in the arbor of *Dans le restaurant* and *The Waste Land*, Section I, where the rain beat; and the moment in the draughty church at smokefall of *The Waste Land* and *Little Gidding*.

The opening lines of Section II of *Burnt Norton* have proven the most puzzling to a number of critics: "Garlic and sapphires in the mud/Clot the bedded axle-tree." In *Burbank with a Baedeker*, Eliot wrote, "The horses, under the axle-tree/Beat up the dawn from Istria/With even feet." Though Venetian frescoes were the immediate literal referent in *Burbank*, both passages seem to suggest the chariot of the sun and the wheeling of the days and seasons. Hugh Kenner speculates that "The axle-tree appears to be that of the turning heavens, its lower end, like the bole of Yggdrasill, embedded in our soil."[6] In Milton's "On the Morning of Christ's Nativity" we read that at the birth of Christ "The sun himself withheld his wonted speed,/And hid his head for shame,/As his inferior flame/The new-enlightened world no more should need;/He saw a greater sun appear/Than his bright throne or burning axle-tree could bear."

In this light, Eliot's daring imagery suggests a parallel between the incarnation of the Word in Christ's birth and the moment of illumination in which the total pattern is grasped. Garlic suggests the human and sapphires the divine natures in either the mud of the "handful of dust" that is man or the mud of the stable of Bethlehem; at any rate, the glory of the incarnation slows the chariot of the sun; clots the axle-tree, making it move more slowly; and draws together all things in a newly perceived pattern. Read with the hindsight of familiarity with *The Family Reunion,* "The trilling wire in the blood" that "Sings below inveterate scars" suggests the family curse, the understanding of which frees Harry and Agatha for their moment of new illumination; and it is this understanding that "reconciles forgotten wars" (for example, the English Civil War of *Little Gidding,* Part III).

The remainder of Part II explores in relatively simple terms the still point where past and future are gathered, the moment of illumination. So Part II has given us "variations on a theme."

Part III considers the two ways suggested by the second epigraph from Heraclitus: the way up and the way down to the moment of illumination. An incomplete version of the way down is explored first in the London subway imagery that recurs in *East Coker.* In the first half of Part III are echoed the "unreal city" sections of *The Waste Land,* and also of *The Hollow Men,* showing us again the "trimmers" who are "distracted from distraction by distraction" on the bank of "the tumid river." This semi-darkness of the twittering subway world is not the vacancy of the mystic's negative approach to illumination, which requires, as we see in the last half of Part III, that we descend lower into "the world of perpetual solitude." This descent is comparable to the devouring by the leopards in Part II of *Ash-Wednesday,* and again the three spirits of Dante's *Vita Nuova* are suggested in the triad "Desiccation of the world of sense,/Evacuation of the world of fancy,/Inoperancy of the world of spirit." This is the way down, and the way up, we are told, is the same. It consists in the action of the saint who is involved in the experience of the world but who, like Thomas in *Murder in the Cathedral,* succeeds in divesting himself of his own will—or rather succeeds in conforming his will to that of God so that he no longer tries to turn the wheel but rests at the still center.

Part IV brings us briefly back to the garden of Part I. "Time and the bell have buried the day." This is the evening bell, and the black cloud that passes "carries the sun away." The questions "Will the sunflower turn to us, will the clematis/Stray down, bend to us; tendril and spray/Clutch and cling?/Chill /Fingers of yew be curled/Down on us?" suggests the *Waste Land* passage "What are the roots that clutch, what branches grow/Out of this stony rubbish?" Several critics have suggested that the sunflower, clematis, and yew represent Christ, the Virgin Mary, and God the Father, and that the kingfisher of Part IV is the Fisher King after whose redemption follows illumination. As in each of the other quartets, Part IV is a brief lyric.

Part V clarifies the nature of the rose-garden moment by emphasis on pattern in music and speech, including poetry. The attempt to find the meaning is always attacked by voices of temptation, by the distractions of involvement with the life of the senses. We are told that "Only by the form, the pattern,/Can words or music reach/The stillness," and the stillness is the conception of the total pattern of the music, though we can hear it only one note at a time, or of the poem, though we hear it only one word at a time. When deeply enough understood, it becomes (as in *The Dry Salvages*) "music heard so deeply/That it is not heard at all, but you are the music/While the music lasts."

The second section of Part V relates this concept of pattern to the rose-garden moment. "The detail of the pattern" may be seen in "the figure of the ten stairs" of the Christian mystic St. John of the Cross and his negative approach to illumination. We have then the contrast between the desire that operates in time and is movement and the love that operates in eternity and is itself unmoving, though it is the cause and the end of all movement. And when, "sudden in a shaft of sunlight," one has seen the view of eternity, then all else, we are told, seems only "the waste sad time/Stretching before and after." And as Grover Smith says,

> . . . an achieved artistic form is not only prolonged but timeless. As a form, a poem or music continues to exist, but also it has always existed and always will exist, both by "the co-existence" of time eternally present and by the eternal status, out of time, of the unmoved actuality that the form mirrors. . . . The final cause precedes the efficient cause just as the completion of a poem, because it moves the beginning, precedes that; and both are simultaneous. So God as final cause, the Omega, is the Alpha or first cause. Thus to Eliot the theme of poetry itself "reaches/Into the silence" to become contemplation of God. The poet, returning to the world of movement, to the writing of these lines, comments next on the task of molding the flux into patterns. . . . the Word that was in the beginning is the Logos, the complete meaning, the pure actuality, unyielding to change. The Word is the perfection moving the poem and the poet too, in his own empty desert.[7]

Thus the link between the poet's task and the quester's task: Each is the quest for the Word.

II East Coker

As the author explained in a letter written shortly after the poem, "The title [*East Coker*] is taken from a village in Somerset where my family lived for some two centuries. The first section contains some phrases in Tudor English taken from 'The Governour' of Sir Thomas Elyot who was a grandson of Simon Elyot or Eliot of that village. The third section contains several lines adapted from 'The Ascent of Mount Carmel.'"[8] He also indicates the likelihood of influence by Gerstärker's *Germelshausen*. Other relevant sources are the motto of Mary Queen of Scots, "*En ma fin est mon commencement*" ("In my end is my beginning"), and the Eliot motto "*tace et fac*" ("Be silent and act"), which, as Elizabeth Drew points out, "could be interpreted as the same as 'We must be still and still moving.'"[9] Good Friday also is relevant to this poem, for Eliot published it on Good Friday, 1940, and referred at the end of Part IV to Christ's Passion and the Eucharist: "Again, in spite of that, we call this Friday good."

Returning to visit the home of his ancestors, as Eliot did in 1937, the poet seeks his beginnings. In poetry reminiscent of Book I of Lucretius' *De rerum natura*, he considers the recurrent cycles of time to which he will, like his ancestors, be subject. He associates the decay of the houses and people in imagery that again, as in *Gerontion*, echoes Ecclesiastes:

> Old stone to new building, old timber to new fires,
> Old fires to ashes, and ashes to the earth
> Which is already flesh, fur and faeces,
> Bone of man and beast, cornstalk and leaf.
> Houses live and die: there is a time for building
> And a time for living and for generation
> And a time for the wind to break the loosened pane
> And to shake the wainscot where the field-mouse trots
> And to shake the tattered arras woven with a silent motto.

The second strophe of Part I recreates his approach to the village; the third, the life of the people who once lived there, dancing happily "in clumsy shoes,/Earth feet, loam feet, lifted in country mirth/. . . Keeping the rhythm in their dancing/As in their living in the living seasons." The poetry is warm and lucid, full of movement. The rhythm of the dance is continued in the movement of the sea, the wind, the day: "Out at sea the dawn wind/Wrinkles and slides." The poet is "here/Or there, or elsewhere. In [his] beginning."

Part II of *East Coker* is an attempt to understand the significance of the pattern—a rational questioning of what it adds up to. But this mode of exploration is "not very satisfactory," and no satisfying answers to the questions of the first strophe emerge. When the details of time are marshalled and put into an equation, they seem to cancel one another out rather than adding up to a pattern. Late November fights spring; summer heat and snowdrops, destructive fire and the ice-cap, all whirl in a vortex. The attempt to arrive by such means at the still moment of knowledge of the pattern is doomed to failure like the "hollyhocks that aim too high/Red into grey and tumble down. . . ." Starting again, the poet echoes Gerontion's disillusionment with the knowledge derived from experience, knowledge which "imposes a pattern, and falsifies." Such attempts at understanding are constantly shifting: new patterns emerge in each moment, "And every moment is a new and shocking/Valuation of all we have been." This is man's fate, and it is not only *"Nel mezzo del cammin di nostra vita"* ("In the middle of the way of our life") but "all the way" that we find ourselves in a dark wood as Dante did. And the approach through knowledge is rejected: "The only wisdom we can hope to acquire/Is the wisdom of humility: humility is endless." Like the dancers and houses, we too shall disappear; but in the surrender to the still point of the turning world, the humble acceptance of Love for the Word that is and was in the beginning, lies the achievement of the saint or the moment in the rose-garden that *is* for Eliot a satisfactory way of putting it.

Part III continues and transmutes this disillusionment with the inevitable passing of all houses and people, all of whom, even if not—like Milton's Samson—blinded for their lust, go into the dark: "O dark dark dark." All of them, like Gerontion's de Bailhache, Fresca, and Mrs. Cammel, are "whirled/Beyond the circuit of the shuddering Bear/In fractured atoms" into "the vacant interstellar spaces." So, in contemplating this village, the poet says to himself, "Be still, and let the dark come upon you/Which shall be the darkness of God." This darkness is the humility which can surrender the rational modes, the efforts to turn the wheel—which can surrender even the hope, love, and faith that would be misguided, since it must be the gift of grace which can neither be forced nor earned. When that surrender is achieved, then come the freeing images of the rose-garden moment:

> Whisper of running streams, and winter lightning.
> The wild thyme unseen and the wild strawberry,
> The laughter in the garden, echoed ecstasy
> Not lost, but requiring, pointing to the agony
> Of death and birth.

In such surrender is the reconciliation of time with the eternal pattern, the merging of word and Word, power and Power (see *Ash-Wednesday*, V). The final strophe of Part III says the same thing again in the terms of St. John of the Cross, describing the way down to mystic union with God.

Part IV renders in Christian and Dantean terms, and especially in the imagery of Good Friday, the combined positive and negative ways, the way up and the way down, fused inseparably. The "illness" of the poet and reader is questioned by the probe wielded by the bleeding, nail-torn hands of Christ. This probing resolves the enigma of unsatisfactory actions in time motivated by the dissatisfaction of the patient and reflected on the fever chart. It is this dissatisfaction, the disease, of which the church, "the dying nurse," reminds us; and it is only the disease—the awareness of unsatisfactoriness—that can, if it grows bad enough, point us toward the final cure. Our hospital, the earth, is endowed not only by Adam, who invented the disease, but chiefly by Christ, the ruined millionaire who gave up heavenly glory to make possible the treatment and cure. And if we are fortunate, the disease will become so bad that we die of it: become dead to the involvement in the transient things of whose unsatisfactoriness God's universal and inescapable scheme continually reminds us—if we do well. As infatuation with the life in time dies out, the chill ascends as it did for Socrates in Plato's *Phaedo* "from feet to knees" and "the fever sings" as it did for Agatha and Harry in *The Family Reunion* "in mental wires." The sickness grows so bad that something must happen: the purgational suffering that leads to a new orientation must be not only accepted but sought, so that the Furies may be transmuted into the Eumenides of Sophocles' *Oedipus at Colonus*, "the All-seeing Kindly Ones."

According to the sections of the *Bhagavad-Gita* that Eliot uses in the *Four Quartets*, it is chiefly wrath and lust that must thus be overcome; and, as the sections of Dante's purgatory in which those sins are purged are approached, it is the smoke and suffering that are first seen; these are the painful briars that one would wish to escape. But when through the almost impossible act of the will (possible only through grace) the purging flame has been entered—the flame that probes the distempered part and burns away the last residue of wrong orientation of love—then "the flame is roses" and nothing is desired more, since nothing else leads to the only thing worth desire, to the Primal Love of which Dante says at the end of *Paradiso*, "Such at that light doth man become that to turn thence to any other sight could not by possibility be ever yielded."[10]

In Canto XXV of *Purgatorio* Dante hears the spirits in the fire singing the *Summae Deus clementiae*, one verse of which, according to Dorothy Sayers, runs, "Burn with meet fires our reins and our sick hearts . . . that having put off evil lusts we may keep watch with loins girded."[11] They also cry out examples of chastity and virtue, and the canto ends: "And this fashion I think suffices them for all the time the fire burns them: with such treatment, and with such diet, must the last wound be healed."[12] This wound suggests the disease in Eliot's earthly hospital, as well as the wounds of lust to the spirit and the *P* (standing for "*Peccata*" or "sin") that has been carved on the forehead of Dante by the angel who admitted him to purgatory, the last of the *P*'s to be erased through the three purgative steps of confession, contrition, and satisfaction.

Eliot's "frigid purgatorial fires" reverse those of Dante, who said, "And I, being in, would have been glad to throw myself for coolness into molten glass, with such unmeasured heat did that fire glow." The acrid, gritty smoke in which wrath is purged is encountered by Dante in the passage where Marco Lombardo explains to Dante (Canto XVI) the nature of the soul and free will in the passage echoed by Eliot's *Animula*. Eliot's reversal of the heat suggests the destructive fire that "burns before the ice-cap reigns" in Part II of *East Coker*, a metaphor for the resolution of opposites that is possible not through logic but in the revelations of the rose-garden moment and in the illumination of the saint. The final five-line strophe of Part IV gives the Good Friday analogy for this purgatorial state, in which the dripping blood and the bloody flesh of the sacrament of communion are our only drink and food. In spite of our normal deluded tendencies, we recognize in these the insubstantiality of flesh and blood—our own—and the primacy of Christ's flesh and blood (the incarnation of divinity in man); and we call the day of crucifixion Good Friday.

Part V of *East Coker* is an intensely personal consideration of the poet's own history and of his changed awareness of his direction and significance. In it he is "in the middle way," still "on the edge of a grimpen," having spent twenty years as poet trying to reconcile the word with the Word; twenty years raiding the inarticulate "with shabby equipment always deteriorating/In the general mess of imprecision of feeling"; trying to find, "By strength and submission, [what] has already been discovered/Once or twice, or several times, by men whom one cannot hope/To emulate" (Shakespeare, Dante, and the writers of the *Bhagavad-Gita,* perhaps); and trying to do all this "under conditions/That seem unpropitious." But perhaps his lot is no worse than theirs was; perhaps the changes in language and in modes of awareness and environment represent neither gain nor loss. As Krishna will tell us in other words in Part III of *The Dry Salvages,* "For us, there is only the trying. The rest is not our business."

And now in the last strophe of *East Coker* is recorded a very significant shift from the attitude of *Burnt Norton* toward the moment of revelation. The effect of growing old is to make the world stranger and its "pattern more complicated/Of dead and living. Not the intense moment/Isolated, with no before and after,/But a lifetime burning in every moment/And not the lifetime of one man only/But of old stones that cannot be deciphered." As this happens, here and now cease to matter and love becomes "most nearly itself." For these reasons old men ought to be explorers; they have learned "to care and not to care," to "be still and still moving/Into another intensity." These lines suggest the successive expansions of Dante's awareness in the *Divine Comedy,* for, at first blinded by the greater brightness of each succeeding angel of the cornices of purgatory, he is later able to look at the ever-increasing brightness of Beatrice, of each new heaven, later of St. Bernard and then of the Virgin Mary, and finally of the Godhead itself. Such a destination can be reached even through "the dark cold and the empty desolation" and "the vast waters" of Gerontion's conclusion. In the light of these new awarenesses, the poet can say with simplicity and conviction that "In my end"—in these new awarenesses and orientations—"is my [real] beginning."

One further point needs to be emphasized before leaving *East Coker*: the inadequacy of "understanding" that Eliot emphasizes in this poem can easily be "understood" as the poem is read and then ignored in the summing up or in afterthoughts on the poem. Eliot echoes the lesson built into every canto of Dante's *Divine Comedy*, the lesson that knowing is a partial mode of awareness, and that simply to "understand" is of little benefit unless the awareness penetrates to the unconscious motives and to the heart and the muscles—unless the unpremeditated action is altered in its quality by an inner change in the whole psyche. It is this awareness that has drawn Eliot throughout his career to the Elizabethan dramatists and to the Metaphysical poets. And though I may have talked in this chapter as though the illumination of the rose-garden moment and of the saint were mental acts, if they are no more than that they are nothing. This is implicit in *East Coker*. And such awareness is what age adds to our rereadings of the great masters "if we do well."

III   The Dry Salvages

To the *air* which stirred the dust on the bowl of rose leaves in *Burnt Norton* and to the soil or *earth* of *East Coker,* the third quartet, *The Dry Salvages*, adds another of the four elements of Heraclitus: the *water* of the river and the ocean. Again, the poem takes its title from the name of a specific place. As Eliot tells us in a note following the title, "(The Dry Salvages—presumably *les trois sauvages*—is a small group of rocks, with a beacon, off the N.E. coast of Cape Ann, Massachusetts. *Salvages* is pronounced to rhyme with *assuages*. . . .)"

Part I of the poem contrasts the river which is within us and the sea which is all about us. The rhythm of the masculine "strong brown god" of the river "was present in the nursery bedroom" in St. Louis; and, though it suggests the life in time with its concomitant limitations, it is the "reminder/Of what men choose to forget." Though in one sense it contrasts with the sea, which is not flowing but universally coexistent, at another level its reminder parallels and its rhythms and cycles parallel the larger pattern of which the sea as well is a part. Through its many voices and its "time not our time," "Older than the time of chronometers, older/Than time counted by anxious worried women/Lying awake, calculating the future,/Trying to unweave, unwind, unravel/And piece together the past and the future,/Between midnight and dawn," these latent suggestions deposit salt on the briar rose and fog in the fir trees. As in *Marina,* this imagery suggests the felicity of the moment of awareness, measureless felicity. This dichotomy of river and sea can be transcended in the glimpse of the over-all pattern.

The first stanza of Part II of *The Dry Salvages* names some of the forms of agony that are a part of man's life in time and also a part of the eternal scheme: the soundless wailing, the silent withering of flowers, the drifting wreckage, and the prayer of the bone on the beach. These are the results of "the calamitous annunciation" of God to Adam and Eve in Genesis 3:16-19. First God said to Eve, "I will greatly multiply thy sorrow and thy conception; in sorrow thou shalt bring forth children; and thy desire shall be to thy husband, and he shall rule over thee." Then He said to Adam, "Because thou hast hearkened unto the voice of thy wife, and hast eaten of the tree, of which I commanded thee, saying, Thou shalt not eat of it: cursed is the ground for thy sake; in sorrow shalt thou eat of it all the days of thy life; Thorns also and thistles shall it bring forth to thee: and thou shalt eat the herb of the field; In the sweat of thy face shalt thou eat bread, till thou return unto the ground; for out of it wast thou taken: for dust thou art, and unto dust shalt thou return." From this annunciation comes the "fear in a handful of dust" of *The Waste Land* and of *Ash-Wednesday.*

After that annunciation there is no end to "the trailing/ Consequence of further days and hours" for man, or of the speaker's particular days and hours. This section of *The Dry Salvages* mixes personal with general and universal comments, and we need not attempt to sort them out since they all "Point to one end, which is always present." A Gerontion-like figure, having rejected the subtle temptations of history, has renounced what was held as most permanent. "The final addition" to that endless sum is "The unattached devotion" of Gerontion and of Pericles "In a drifting boat with a slow leakage" before the meeting with Marina—"The silent listening to the undeniable/ Clamor of the bell of the last annunciation." Perhaps this is Donne's parting bell, which "tolls for thee," and also the bell clanged by the unhurried ground swell of the time "Older than the time of chronometers" in Part I.

But since Adam's curse there is no end to this recurring cycle of birth, procreation, and death. But what must be attended to in the endless procession of lives is not the fact that their trips, their hauls, will not bear examination, but rather the quality of their action, which makes each life, however humble, as significant as any other. There is no end to all these agonies, no possible redemption from the cycle, except "the hardly, barely prayable/Prayer of the one Annunciation," the annunciation of the incarnation of the Logos in human flesh.

This poetry of the first six strophes of Part II is so trenchant and so moving that it may come as a surprise to realize after a number of readings that it is set in the *sestina* form, in which identical rhymes for each of the six-line stanzas are used and in which the final sixth stanza duplicates exactly the rhyme words of the first. But this is not simply a trick, nor a device of virtuosity; whether consciously noted or not, the echoed rhymes etch the meanings more deeply into the consciousness of the reader.

The second half of Part II alters again, in one long strophe, the significance of the rose-garden experience of *Burnt Norton*. There, everything else seemed "the waste sad time/Stretching before and after," and only the sudden shaft of sunlight seemed worth-while. In *East Coker*, to this conception was added the lifetime "burning in every moment" as one becomes older; and now the poet emphasizes that again the pattern changes, that the past "ceases to be a mere sequence—/Or even development," that the moments of happiness, the sudden illumination of *Burnt Norton*, were not properly understood: "We had the experience but missed the meaning,/And approach to the meaning restores the experience/In a different form, beyond any meaning/We can assign to happiness." But "Now, we come to discover that the moments of agony," as well as the moments of felicity, "are likewise permanent/With such permanence as time has. We appreciate this better/In the agony of others, nearly experienced, . . . For our own past is covered by the currents of action."

And it is to communicate such moments of both agony and felicity that the arts of music and poetry and painting are properly intended. It is this that justifies the life and the career of the artist. These moments of agony and felicity, the picture of the whole pattern, are preserved by time, which destroys each individual life. Each of them, like Eve's bitter apple, is comparable to the **Dry Salvages**:

And the ragged rock in the restless waters,
Waves wash over it, fogs conceal it;
On a halcyon day it is merely a monument,
In navigable weather it is always a seamark
To lay a course by: but in the sombre season
Or the sudden fury, is what it always was.

In this third part of *The Dry Salvages*, once more the past, present, future and the way up and the way down of *Burnt Norton* are considered; but now the emphasis is changed from the passive acceptance of the moment of illumination to the right action of a whole lifetime, without thought of the consequences: "Not fare well,/But fare forward, voyagers."

Part III of *The Dry Salvages* relates what has been discussed so far in the three quartets to the scheme of the *Bhagavad-Gita*. This work ("The Song of God" in the Hindu epic *Mahabharata*) consists chiefly in the dialogue between Arjuna, one of the Pandava princes, and Krishna, a god incarnated as his friend and charioteer. Drawn up in battle against his own relatives, Arjuna has looked around and seen his kinsmen in both armies; and he questions the purposes and the rightness of the battle for which they are prepared. Krishna replies to him by explaining the nature of the Atman, the Godhead within every being which has many links to the view of the total pattern that is the subject of the illumination discussed in the *Four Quartets*. Krishna explains furthermore that the two ways of achieving Brahman are by the renunciation of action and by the performing of action: "Action rightly renounced brings freedom:/Action rightly performed brings freedom:/Both are better/Than mere shunning of action. . . . The wise see knowledge and action as one:/They see truly./Take either path/And tread it to the end: /The end is the same./There the followers of action/Meet the seekers after knowledge/In equal freedom."[13]

In the eighth section of the *Bhagavad-Gita*, "The way to eternal Brahman," from which Eliot takes his quotation of Krishna, are suggested most of the main themes of the *Four Quartets*:

ARJUNA:

Tell me Krishna, what Brahman is. What is the Atman, and what is the creative energy of Brahman? Explain the nature of this relative world, and of the individual man.

Who is God who presides over action in this body, and how does He dwell here? How are you revealed at the hour of death to those whose consciousness is united with you?

SRI KRISHNA:

Brahman is that which is immutable, and independent of any cause but Itself. When we consider Brahman as lodged within the individual being, we call Him the Atman. The creative energy of Brahman is that which causes all existences to come into being.

The nature of the relative world is mutability. The nature of the individual man is his consciousness of ego. I alone am God who presides over action, here in this body.

At the hour of death, when a man leaves his body, he must depart with his consciousness absorbed in me. Then he will be united with me. Be certain of that. Whatever a man remembers at the last, when he is leaving the body, will be realized by him in the hereafter; because that will be what his mind has most constantly dwelt on, during this life.

Therefore you must remember me at all times, and do your duty. If your mind and heart are set upon me constantly, you will come to me. Never doubt this.

Make a habit of practising meditation, and do not let your mind be distracted. In this way you will come finally to the Lord, who is the light-giver, the highest of the high.[14]

Examination of the context of this section of the *Bhagavad-Gita* will illuminate and echo many points in the *Four Quartets* and, indeed, those found elsewhere in Eliot's works as well. The slightly puzzling repeated line of Harry and Agatha in *The Family Reunion,* for instance, "Until the chain breaks," is clarified:

He who sees the inaction that is in action, and the action that is in inaction, is wise indeed. Even when he is engaged in action he remains poised in the tranquillity of the Atman./The seers say truly/That he is wise/Who acts without lust or scheming/For the fruit of the act:/His act falls from him, /Its chain is broken,/Melted in the flame of my knowledge. /Turning his face from the fruit,/He needs nothing:/The Atman is enough./He acts, and is beyond action.[15]

The whole *Bhagavad-Gita* will be found relevant not only to the quartets, but also to *Murder in the Cathedral, Ash-Wednesday, The Family Reunion,* and other of Eliot's works. The tolerance of this religion (as stated by Krishna) is echoed in Eliot's use of imagery from several religions. Krishna tells Arjuna that "it does not matter what deity a devotee chooses to worship. If he has faith, I make his faith unwavering. Endowed with the faith I give him, he worships that deity, and gets from it everything he prays for. In reality, I alone am the giver."[16] No serious student of Eliot's poetry can afford to ignore his early and continued interest in the *Bhagavad-Gita*. No work is more relevant except Dante's *Divine Comedy*.

Part IV is a brief prayer to the Virgin Mary, the Queen of Heaven as invoked in St. Bernard's prayer in *Paradiso* XXXIII, 1, and in *Ash-Wednesday*, II. Bernard prayed that Mary would bring to Dante the grace to enable him to see God; in Part IV of Eliot's work the prayer of Mary is invoked for all "those concerned with every lawful traffic."

Part V enumerates many ways in which "Men's curiosity searches past and future/And clings to that dimension." All that, however, is useless. But only the saint can live constantly at the point of "intersection of the timeless/With time . . . in a lifetime's death in love,/Ardour and selflessness and self-surrender./For most of us, there is only the unattended/Moment, the moment in and out of time,/The distraction fit, lost in a shaft of sunlight." Again the wild thyme, the winter lightning, the waterfall, and "music heard so deeply/That it is not heard at all, but you are the music/While the music lasts" are evoked; but "These are only hints and guesses,/Hints followed by guesses; and the rest/Is prayer, observance, discipline, thought and action./The hint half guessed, the gift half understood ["I sometimes wonder if that is what Krishna meant"], is Incarnation./. . . And right action is freedom/From past and future also." But most of us are not saints, and we "are only undefeated/Because we have gone on trying." Between the rose-garden moments and those of agony we are content if our turning back to the life of time contributes to the making of significant soil, as in *East Coker*.

IV   Little Gidding

Little Gidding was a religious utopian community founded in 1625 in Huntingdonshire. The community, patterned on the Christian family, was founded by Nicholas Ferrar and his family. It was visited by Charles I in 1633 and 1642 and again in 1645 after his defeat at Naseby by Cromwell. Two years later it was attacked and disbanded by Parliament. Its destroyed chapel was later rebuilt, but the community was never re-established. Helen Gardner writes, "An admirable account of the life at Little Gidding can be found in Shorthouse's novel *John*

Inglesant. It is a book of singular charm and refinement of feeling, and all that is necessary for an understanding of what the name of the poem should suggest can be found in it."[17]

Part I of *Little Gidding* gives us—as in each of the other quartets—a literal picture of the place after which the poem is named and of the approach to it; but this picture has more than the literal level of meaning. The poet approaches in "midwinter spring," the season "when the day is brightest . . . in the dark time of year." The blossoms on the hedgerow are the transitory ones of snow, and this season is "not in the scheme of generation," but blazes with pentecostal fire. This light contrasts with the darkness of the three earlier quartets, and it also suggests the blinding light, increasing in intensity, as Dante ascends the Mount of Purgatory and then through the successive heavens to the final brightness of the vision of God.

This light, this springtime, is not in time but in eternity, in the illumination of the saint, and in the knowledge of the Atman. And though the poet approached Little Gidding for conscious reasons, he finds that, as he turns off the road "behind the pig-sty to the dull façade/And the tombstone," his conscious purpose dissolves. He finds himself at the world's end—at a place where prayer has been valid, as in all of the places where the saints and martyrs stood. He finds new understanding of the meaning of this place: "And what the dead had no speech for, when living,/They can tell you, being dead: the communication/Of the dead is tongued with fire beyond the language of the living." In this hallowed spot, "the intersection of the timeless moment" becomes "England and nowhere, Never and always." Such a place—whenever, however, and for whatever reason approached—can bring the servant of time in touch with the eternal; and the contemplation of the significant lives which contributed to this significant soil can enable him to escape his own enchainment to time.

Part II re-evaluates everything that has come before in the quartets; it considers the death of air, of earth, of water and fire—the Heraclitean elements respectively associated with the four poems—and it surrenders the significance of each of them in turn. The air in which the dust of *Burnt Norton* was suspended and the dust of the houses and people of *East Coker* remind us of the mortality of man, his works, his homes; this is the death of air. And in spite of all our toil, our works, we are soon gone and the parched, cracked desert is left showing the vanity of our accomplishments; this is the death of earth. And the water and fire that burn and rot man's accomplishments, as well as the things that he refused to attend to, bring the death of water and fire, as in *The Dry Salvages* and *Little Gidding*.

Next follows what is justly Eliot's most admired passage of poetry, the Dantesque meeting with the "familiar compound ghost" who treads the London pavement with him in a dead patrol at the end of an air raid—the passage that Eliot says cost him more effort and difficulty than any other passage of similar length that he has written. Here, in London during the blitz of the Stuka incendiary bomb raids, the block warden tramping "Between three districts whence the smoke arose" meets his ghost, "Both intimate and unidentifiable." Nothing daunted by that disclaimer, the critics have variously identified the ghost as Browning, Yeats, Mallarmé, Hamlet's father, Ezra Pound, Dante, Swift, Milton, Brunetto Latini, and others; but none and yet many of these identifications are correct.

It seems to me that in this ghost the poet meets himself—his earlier self, as influenced by the various dead masters. Certainly the meeting with Brunetto Latini in circle seven of the *Inferno* is unmistakably evoked in the "brown baked features" seen here, but if Eliot is following that account, his protagonist himself first takes the part of Brunetto and looks up into his own down-turned face with "That pointed scrutiny with which we challenge/The first-met stranger in the waning dusk." Immediately, however, we find him up on the raised margin of the river (looking down at his own brown-baked features) from which he peered upward a moment before (catching the look of some dead master).

But the debts reflected in the face are both intimate and unidentifiable. Later, in *The Confidential Clerk*, Colby Simpkins says,

> . . . from time to time, when I least expect it,
> When my mind is cleared and empty, walking in the street
> Or waking in the night, then the former person,
> The person I used to be, returns to take possession:
> And I am again the disappointed organist,
> And for a moment the thing I cannot do,
> The art that I could never excel in,
> Seems the one thing worth doing, the one thing
> That I want to do.
> I have to fight that person.

To this statement Sir Claude Mulhammer replies, "I understand what you are saying/Much better than you think. It's my
own experience/That you are repeating."[18]

So the poet himself in *Little Gidding* assumes "a double part"
crying, and hearing another's voice cry, "'What! are *you* here?'
/Although [they] were not." He "was still the same,/Knowing
[himself], yet being someone other—/And he a face still form-
ing." Like Shelley's Magus Zoroaster, as quoted in *The Cocktail
Party*, he has met his own image walking not in the garden
but in the unreal city of London. He urges his former self to
speak, warning that "'I may not comprehend, may not remember'"; and that former self, as he now understands it,
replies:

> And he [*"ed egli"*]: 'I am not eager to rehearse.
>   My thought and theory which you have forgotten.
>   These things have served their purpose: let them be.
> So with your own, and pray they be forgiven
>   By others, as I pray you to forgive
>   Both bad and good. . . .
>
> . . . .
>
>   For last year's words belong to last year's language
>   And next year's words await another voice.'

Now that the proper steps have been taken, now that the
speaker has escaped from his former to his present self, the
passage to peace for the troubled, departed spirit no longer
presents any hindrance "To the spirit unappeased and peregrine/
Between two worlds become much like each other." We may
compare Elpenor in the *Odyssey* and the ghost of Hamlet's
father. The hell of wartime London is not very different from
the tortures to which the ghost of Hamlet's father is subjected.

Since the concern of both the former and the present self
was speech, the former self volunteers to "disclose the gifts
reserved for age": the "cold friction of expiring sense," the
"impotence of rage/At human folly," and "the laceration/Of
laughter at what ceases to amuse./And last, the rending pain
of re-enactment/Of all that you have done, and been," with its
"new and shocking/Valuation of all we have been," as in Part II
of *East Coker*. After those re-evaluations, "Then fools' approval
stings, and honour stains,/From wrong to wrong the exasperated

spirit/Proceeds, unless restored by that refining fire/Where you must move in measure, like a dancer," acting, not passive. With that revelation, the former self fades as the all-clear siren sounds. In this short section of unrhymed *terza rima*, anyone familiar with Dante will recognize dozens of echoes. This is probably the most successfully Dantesque poetry in English.

Part III discusses "three conditions which often look alike/ Yet differ completely . . ./Attachment to self and to things and to persons, detachment/From self and from things and from persons; and, growing between them, indifference/Which resembles the others as death resembles life . . ./This is the use of memory: /For liberation—not less of love but expanding/Of love beyond desire, and so liberation/From the future as well as the past." This liberation suggests the expansion of desire for the earthly Beatrice into love for the final cause; and it suggests also, as in the *Bhagavad-Gita,* the freedom, the knowledge of Atman that grows out of either right action or right renunciation of action— "unflowering, between/The live and the dead nettle." Both action and renunciation, we are told there, are better than the mere shunning of action, like that of Dante's trimmers and of Eliot's hollow men. What is needed is not laziness, but the disinterestedness of one who has traveled either the way up or the way down.

Relaxing to a more literal awareness of the Little Gidding setting, the poet considers those who figured in its history: Ferrar and those associated with his community and those who attacked and scattered it—those "not wholly commendable" on both sides of a Civil War. He thinks of King Charles and of those who were executed on the scaffold during the war, and of saints who died in various places and "one who died blind and quiet," possibly Oedipus at Colonus or Milton or James Joyce, or Gerontion. We "celebrate/These dead men more than the dying [of World War II]," but this is not to say that the past is better than the present nor to summon the irrecoverable "spectre of a Rose" of Dante and the Middle Ages, not to revive old factions or policies; all of them "are folded in a single party," and what we get from the tradition, we get from all of them, friend and foe alike. When we can grasp it, they are symbols perfected in death; if we can grasp it, then, as Dame Julian of Norwich wrote, "all shall be well."

Part IV sets in parallel the incendiary bombs of the German Stuka bombers and the pentecostal fire of the descending dove.

These "tongues declare/The one discharge from sin and error."
We must choose either fire or fire—the burning fire of lust of
St. Augustine or the purging fire of Arnaut Daniel, as was made
clear in "The Fire Sermon," Part III of *The Waste Land*. The
last strophe of *Little Gidding*, Part IV, parallels Part IV of
East Coker, reminding us that Love "prevents us everywhere"
and that the fever will consume us unless we dive into the
cleansing fire, where we "must move in measure, like a dancer."

In Part V of *Little Gidding* the strands of the poem are all
drawn together, and the advances of each quartet over the
previous ones are consolidated. Especially the necessity of acting, of continuing the exploring urged in *The Dry Salvages*, is
reiterated with the promise of the right results. The poet once
more examines his poetic craft, the various endings and beginnings that he has made as poet, and the struggle to find the
right word to stimulate knowledge of the Word. The ideal
speech of contemporary poetry is memorably described:

> And every phrase
> And sentence that is right (where every word is at home,
> Taking its place to support the others,
> The word neither diffident nor ostentatious,
> An easy commerce of the old and the new,
> The common word exact without vulgarity,
> The formal word precise but not pedantic,
> The complete consort dancing together)

This is the proper action of the poet; and every poem or other
action properly performed is as significant as the actions of the
figures who make history meaningful. In the light of right
action we understand the significance of them all: "We die with
the dying. . . . We are born with the dead." And now, while
the light falls on the secluded chapel at Little Gidding, "History
is now and England"—in the proper pentecostal light of this
quartet. Asserting the intent of exploring to the last beginning,
"the source of the longest river"—and this time the meaning will
not be missed—the poet voices "A condition of complete
simplicity/(Costing not less than everything)," and he closes his
poem on an evocation of Dante's final vision of God:

> Oh grace abounding, wherein I presumed to fix
> my look on the eternal light so long that I
> wearied my sight thereon!

> Within its depths I saw ingathered, bound by
>   love in one volume, the scattered leaves of
>   all the universe;
> Substance and accidents and their relations, as
>   though together fused, after such fashion that
>   what I tell of is one simple flame.[19]

When this ingathering is achieved, "all shall be well and/All manner of thing shall be well." And after mirroring in his own terms this passage of *Paradiso* XXXIII, which to his "thinking [is] the highest point that poetry has ever reached or ever can reach," Eliot turned to the action of drama and wrote no more poetry in such a mode. And, indeed, what more was there to say?

CHAPTER 8

The Tougher Self

ELIOT WROTE in 1933, "The ideal medium for poetry, to my mind, and the most direct means of social 'usefulness' for poetry, is the theatre."[1] In *The Cocktail Party*, Eliot entered the popular, competitive commercial theatre and his play was a stunning success—one unmatched by any other serious verse play of the twentieth century. By this time (1949) Eliot, allying his verse to the rhythms of modern English speech, had adopted his flexible three-stress-and-a-caesura line and had brought it to such perfection of control that he could modulate in it from the most prosaic-sounding lines to high moments of intense poetry.

I The Cocktail Party

Several themes of his less universally acclaimed plays— martyrdom and the search for identity and vocation, for example —survive in *The Cocktail Party*; but the terms and the imagery of the play largely avoid an exclusively Christian (or even explicitly Christian) frame of reference. And in this play attention was focused not chiefly on the potential saint but on a group of seven characters of varying potentialities. And for the first time, the characters capable only of humbler choices are given as much emphasis as, or more than, the potential saint. Sparkingly humorous, the play is yet unmistakably a serious comedy, one which makes the audience quite aware of meanings behind those which immediately emerge. Because the enthusiasm of commentators for the play has led a number of them to advance all sorts of speculations about the tantalizing questions that grow out of it, and because of its relevance to my basic approaches to Eliot's whole poetic production, *The Cocktail Party* will be given fuller treatment in this study than any of the other plays.

The play opens on a cocktail party in the flat of Edward
Chamberlayne, a lawyer, and his wife Lavinia, who is not present. After seemingly typical party chit-chat during which
Edward explains that Lavinia was suddenly called away to
visit a sick aunt, the guests all leave except one; he is designated
simply as the Unidentified Guest. As they have another drink,
Edward tells him that actually Lavinia has left him and that he
would like to have her back. After suggesting that Edward and
Lavinia are probably better off apart, the stranger mysteriously
promises to bring her back the next day. They are interrupted
by the return of Julia Shuttlethwaite, a garrulous lady who
pretends to have forgotten her umbrella; the Unidentified Guest
leaves; Julia returns a second time looking for her glasses,
accompanied by Peter Quilpe, a young writer who was also at
the party. Finding her glasses in her purse, Julia leaves; and
Peter then asks Edward to help him win Celia Coplestone. Alex
Gibbs, the one other guest at the cocktail party, also returns
and insists on fixing Edward's dinner.

After Alex and Peter leave, Celia comes in and we learn
that she and Edward have been having an affair. When he tells
Celia he wants Lavinia back, they lose all rapport. Again Julia
appears, this time ostensibly to fix Edward some dinner. After
she leaves, Edward and Celia contemplate the end of their
affair.

The next afternoon, through various confusions, all of them
appear again and Lavinia returns. After the others leave (Celia
permanently and Peter for a job in California), Edward and
Lavinia find each other unbearable.

Act Two is set several weeks later in the consulting room of
Sir Henry Harcourt-Reilly, a psychiatrist who turns out to be
the Unidentified Guest of Act One. He interviews first Edward
alone and then Edward and Lavinia together, making them both
honestly face their true natures and their relations with each
other. They leave together, planning to "make the best of a
bad job." Reilly then interviews Celia, who feels estranged from
the rest of the world; and he agrees to send her, by her own
choice, to his "sanatorium." Act Two closes as Reilly, Julia, and
Alex drink a libation to the success of his prescriptions for the
three patients.

Act Three takes place two years later just before another
cocktail party given by the Chamberlaynes. Again all of the
original guests assemble, except Celia Coplestone; Alex relates

that she has died as a member of a nursing order in a little-known island called Kinkanja. The news of her death enables Edward, Lavinia, and Peter Quilpe to understand better their own natures and the nature of their involvements with Celia and one another. The play ends as the party begins.

Since its 1949 premier, a reasonably accurate and fairly detailed picture of the underlying relationships structuring the play has emerged in various published critiques. Yet a number of troublesome points remain. Primary among these are questions regarding the character and plausibility of Sir Henry Harcourt-Reilly, the suitability of Celia Coplestone's particular death and of Alex' retelling of it, and, indeed, the utility and success of the whole of Act Three with its cocktail party. I suggest that each of these problems arises from a misreading of the psychological—or perhaps better, the "psychic"—content of the play.

Part I Psychic Scheme

As to the basic human problem elucidated by the play, essentially this picture is set forth: Each person, in his relationships with others, has been crusted over with illusions about himself and others; he has developed a personality which is largely false and artificial. Somewhere beneath this facade lies his necessary self. Before he can achieve a meaningful and satisfying life, he must somehow strip away the illusions and recognize his deeper, tougher self. Edward says:

> The self that can say 'I want this—or want that'—
> The self that wills—he is a feeble creature;
> He has to come to terms in the end
> With the obstinate, the tougher self; who does not speak,
> Who never talks, who cannot argue;
> And who in some men may be the *guardian*—
> But in men like me, the dull, the implacable,
> The indomitable spirit of mediocrity.
> The willing self can contrive the disaster
> Of this unwilling partnership—but can only flourish
> In submission to the rule of the stronger partner.

The nature of one's tougher self is not his responsibility; he may have the potentialities of a saint, like Celia, or his destiny may lie in some other direction, as do those of Edward, Lavinia, Reilly, Julia, and Alex. At any rate, he must discover and come to terms with his basic role—his "destiny." The purpose of Reilly, Julia, and Alex is to help the other characters strip away their illusions and make their decisions. Julia says of Edward and Lavinia, after they have left Reilly's office:

> All we could do was to give them the chance.
> And now, when they are stripped naked to their souls
> And can choose, whether to put on proper costumes
> Or huddle quickly into new disguises,
> They have, for the first time, somewhere to start from.

Not all people can strip themselves clean of their illusions. Peter Quilpe, for example, does not reach that point in the play; but he shows promise at the end that he may reach it soon. The guardian trio, Reilly and his associates, have successfully completed this step in the soul's itinerary before the play begins; though wholly human, they are able to guide the Chamberlaynes and Celia, in the second act, to that same moment.

The stripping away of illusions is a painful process; the identity one has to face may not fit at all with dearly held notions of oneself. Each person, Reilly says, must learn that all other people are strangers, and that we are strangers even to ourselves. Only in the illusory personality do we normally conceive of our identities, and our views of others are equally or perhaps even more erroneous. Once our illusions are shed, the lack of them seems at first an intolerable isolation; but Reilly impresses on Edward the fact that we are always and only strangers, and he urges him and Lavinia to see their isolation as the bond which could hold them together. Each person can and must make decisions; once made, however, these decisions set in motion forces in one's own life and in the lives of others which cannot be altered. Our freedom is limited by our previous choices and our involvement with others and also by the nature and workings of our unknown selves.

Since the illusory personality is built up in social relationships, the stripping away of illusion is usually a concomitant of the breaking-up of those relationships. In Edward's case the awareness follows on Lavinia's departure, Peter's reminder of his age, and Edward's recognizing the falsity of his former relation to Celia. Lavinia's enlightenment hinges on the breakdown of her relationships with Peter and Edward. Each of the Chamberlaynes has to be prodded into self-recognitions by Reilly; Celia, on the other hand, is inherently honest with herself, and works out her own salvation with only hints and good will from Reilly—who is, in any case, incapable of understanding her nature and destiny except in vague and second-hand terms. Celia's self-discovery grows out of her recognizing her misconceptions of Edward and their affair. She immediately realizes what Edward and Lavinia grasp firmly only at the end of the play: that her pictures of the persons with whom she was involved have been only projected desires, not the real persons. She tells Edward, for example, that she has looked at him now and seen nothing left but a beetle. When Edward says, "Perhaps that is what I am./Tread on me, if you like," Celia replies:

> No, I won't tread on you.
> That is not what you are. It is only what was left
> Of what I had thought you were. I see another person,
> I see you as a person whom I never saw before.
> The man I saw before, he was only a projection—
> I see that now—of something that I wanted—
> No, not *wanted*—something I aspired to—

Thus the loss of illusions about other persons painfully reveals our tendency to project on others both our own ideas of them and our own needs. This dawning awareness stimulates the recognition of one's misconceptions of himself as well.

What follows this confrontation of oneself depends on one's moral acumen and the nature of the tougher self which is discovered. At this point most of the play's commentators have gone astray by assuming the play to state that every person has a choice between Celia's way of sainthood and Edward's making "the best of a bad job" (Edward's summary of his and Lavinia's destiny). This assumption is not accurate. The dilemma facing each person after he loses his illusions and confronts his tougher self is that stated by Julia above: "whether to put on proper costumes/Or huddle quickly into new disguises." This is the crucial choice, as Lavinia sensed when she told Edward that the change that comes from seeing oneself through the eyes of other people "must have been very shattering for you./But never mind, you'll soon get over it/And find yourself another little part to play,/With another face, to take people in." And without the proddings of Reilly, that is just what both Edward and Lavinia would have done.

For almost all persons, the mystic way of sainthood is not even a remote possibility; and it is to be thought of not as one of the two normally available alternatives, but as an extreme on the very wide scale of possibilities for those who, like Edward, Lavinia, Celia, Reilly, Julia, and Alex, have chosen "to put on proper costumes." Those who "huddle quickly into new disguises" or who, like Peter Quilpe after the revelations attending the first cocktail party, have not yet lost all illusions, can neither become saints nor "make the best of a bad job." But there is hope that they may later, at the low point of another cycle of "the machine" of human interrelations, be stripped clean of illusions and have another chance to choose; Peter seems at the end of the play to be approaching such a time of decision. Further, the following important speech of Reilly almost negates the phrase "a bad job": "When you find, Mr. Chamberlayne,/The best of a bad job is all any of us make of it—/Except of course, the saints—such as those who go/To the sanatorium—you will forget this phrase./And in forgetting it will alter the condition." The negative view of "the human condition" implicit in the phrase "a bad job" is Edward's; it is not the author's or Reilly's. This speech is closely related to Julia's reminder to Reilly that he must accept his limitations.

Some detractors interpret too narrowly and too negatively Reilly's statement that those who become reconciled to "the human condition"

> Maintain themselves by the common routine,
> Learn to avoid excessive expectation,
> Become tolerant of themselves and others,
> Giving and taking, in the usual actions
> What there is to give and take. They do not repine;
> Are contented with the morning that separates
> And with the evening that brings together
> For casual talk before the fire
> Two people who know they do not understand each other,
> Breeding children whom they do not understand
> And who will never understand them.

Readers who see in this pattern only "dull grayness" and abstracted inhumanity have imposed limitations of meaning that the play does not justify. Reilly comments on the range of his clientele (and of the characters in *The Cocktail Party*) in his interview with the Chamberlaynes: "I do not trouble myself with the common cheat,/Or with the insuperably, innocently dull:/My patients such as you are the self-deceivers/

Taking infinite pains, exhausting their energy,/Yet never quite successful." Presumably those who do not deceive themselves might achieve felicity of various sorts without ever coming under the purview of such a one as Reilly; they would probably be found in other circles than those in which he operates; the suggestion that we are seeing the limited cocktail set picture is implicit throughout the play, if never totally explicit. Perhaps we should see in Reilly's song a suggestion that, in the areas in which the play operates, edifying sexual relationships are rare or—for some—impossible.

Eliot neither pretends nor implies that the characters in this play represent the complete range of human possibilities. That they do not is patent. They do, however, convincingly and dramatically represent people who might well associate on such terms as those of the play, and no dramatist can hope to do more. In this comedy, for the first time in his major plays, as we mentioned before, Eliot gives more weight and attention to humanization of non-saints than to the transhumanization of a saint. A turn has been made in his dramaturgic career toward a play without a saint, toward the later *The Elder Statesman*— a play that many critics find much more pleasing than *The Cocktail Party*, though Peter Quilpe, I am certain, would not.

Part II The Guardians

No one person in *The Cocktail Party* stands out above his fellows in importance to the degree that is usual in modern plays. Instead we see two groups of characters. Each is indispensable to the central intent of the work, and each shows among its several characters a range of propensities, traits, and actions which are necessary to the unity. Following the precepts of Aristotle's *Poetics* and the precedent of the great classical dramatists, Eliot has presented his characters only in the dimensions relevant to the life of the drama. This is not to say that they are unsatisfactory or incomplete, but rather that the play is not cluttered with the realistic irrelevancies to which most modern readers and playgoers are only too accustomed. Thus the qualities seen in the characters are so integral to their actions and their relations with others as to lead the attention back immediately to the play's total scheme. The main character is not Edward nor Lavinia, Peter nor Celia, Julia nor Sir Henry Harcourt-Reilly, but all of them. What we may say about any one character, however helpful, is obviously and annoyingly partial in nature. Before considering individuals separately, let us look at the two main groups of characters and their interrelations.

Edward and Lavinia Chamberlayne, Celia Coplestone, and Peter Quilpe make up the first group—each of them struggling to find and accept his destiny. These four are wholly convincing cocktail party characters; each is indispensable to anything approximating a full dramatic development of the play's main themes. It is in the range of these characters, their problems, and their ways of meeting their problems that the central meanings (how individuals can discover and accept their "tougher selves") of the play emerge.

The second group, called "the guardians" by most critics, is made up of Sir Henry Harcourt-Reilly, the garrulous and inquisitive Julia Shuttlethwaite, and Alexander MacColgie Gibbs. These much less ordinary characters suggest the "clerisy" or "charismatic" personalities referred to in Eliot's 1939 essay "The Idea of a Christian Society."

Eliot's use of the term "guardians" in the play, though it occurs in only two brief passages, throws some light on the total scheme of the play. Edward first uses the word in the "tougher self" speech already quoted. After this speech (Julia has left Edward and Celia alone, but has phoned to hurry Celia along and to ask her to bring Julia's spectacles with her), Edward brings into the room the champagne bottle previously found in the kitchen by Julia.

CELIA: Why bring an empty champagne bottle?

EDWARD:
>It isn't empty. It may be a little flat—
>But why did she say that it was a half bottle?
>It's one of my best: and I have no half bottles.
>Well, I hoped you would drink a final glass with me.

CELIA: What should we drink to?

EDWARD: Whom shall we drink to?

CELIA: To the Guardians.

EDWARD: To the Guardians?

CELIA: To the Guardians. It was you who spoke of
>guardians. (*They drink*)
>It may be that even Julia is a guardian.
>Perhaps she is *my* guardian. Give me the spectacles.
>Good night, Edward.

It is true that the tougher selves of Reilly, Julia, and Alex, operating through their influences on the other characters of the play, make them guardians with a lower case "g," and yet there are the upper case Guardians to whom they offer the libations at the end of Act II, invoking the protection of the stars over the Chamberlaynes and asking, "May the holy ones watch over the roof,/May the Moon herself influence the bed." They also invoke for Celia the watchfulness and protection of the "Protector of travellers." There is even the suggestion, before the end of Act III, that Edward and Lavinia are approaching the degree of understanding necessary to help Peter reach the condition in which perhaps the words of the libation scene can be valid for him, and they are thus in a sense also becoming guardians. Given these reservations, we shall use the uncapitalized term "guardians" to refer to Reilly, Julia, and Alex.

The most intriguing of the guardians—indeed, one of the most intriguing dramatic characters to be found in modern drama—is Sir Henry Harcourt-Reilly, who is also the Unidentified Guest of the first act. This astonishing person is referred to in the play as a doctor, but he has been labeled by various critics as a psychoanalyst, a priest, God, an eccentric madman, and, most frequently, simply as a psychiatrist. For instance, Irwin Edman, in a review of the Decca recordings of *The Cocktail Party*, wondered whether it is Eliot or Alec Guinness, cast as Reilly, who makes Sir Henry seem in the recording "so smug, so much God disguised as T. S. Eliot or Eliot disguised as God or God's priest."[2]

The interpretations of Reilly as superhuman stem from several causes. His admonitions to his patients to "Go in peace. And work out your salvation with diligence" have been taken by most critics as showing Reilly to be at least an Anglican priest, if not a member of the divine Trinity. And Christ is strikingly suggested in Reilly's words "It is finished," spoken after Celia has left his office. The libation scene in Act II and the references of the guardians to projected spirits and the process of transhumanization also suggest knowledge of an extra-human sort.

These suggestions, however, may be quickly answered: "Go in peace. And work out your salvation with diligence" is—as more than one critic has shown—the dying statement of Gotama, the Buddha, as translated in a book cited in Eliot's notes to *The Waste Land*; the talk of transhumanization and projected spirits can be explained as neoplatonic occultism or the ritual of a typical secret society. And Reilly's many expressed limitations rob him of credibility as a Christ figure. In an interview for *The New York Times*,[3] Eliot—though on many questions he preferred that the play itself should answer—went so far as to say that Reilly was not intended to represent God, as some reviewers had suggested.

To consider the possibilities of Reilly's superhumanity in another direction, Eliot caps a series of plays on the word "devil" by having Celia say, when Edward tells her that the Unidentified Guest caused him to realize he wanted Lavinia back while seeming to argue against her return, "That's the Devil's method!" The humor in this series of remarks has hinged on the popular tendency to link anyone who manipulates the emotions of others with witchcraft or black magic.

Certainly the suggested links between Reilly and God, Buddha, the Devil, and an Anglican priest have strong connotative values —values which heighten the curiosity of the audience and suggest, in incommensurable ways, the stature of Reilly; but the suggestions attenuate each other. Their chief use perhaps is to demonstrate Reilly's excellent sense of humor. Each of them is, in some particular way, metaphorically potent; but there seems to be no evidence to support a consistent allegorical identification of Reilly, and any reader who takes them too seriously misses some of the play's finest humor.

Certainly at the literal level Eliot takes great care to point out Reilly's humanness and concomitant limitations. In Act II, for example, Reilly expresses misgivings regarding his handling of Edward and Lavinia's problems: "I have taken a great risk." Julia replies, "We must always take risks./That is our destiny. Since you question the decision/What possible alternative can you imagine?" To Reilly's "None," Julia answers, "Very well then. We must take the risk./All we could do was to give them the chance." Later, speaking of Celia, Julia says, "O yes, she will go far. And we know where she is going./But what do we know of the terrors of the journey?/You and I don't know the process by which the human is/Transhumanised: what do we know/Of the kind of suffering they must undergo/On the way of illumination?" And shortly after, Reilly again unmistakably emphasizes his limitations: "And when I say to one like her,/'Work out your salvation with diligence,' I do not understand/What I myself am saying."

None of these elements seems to me in any way to imply

that Reilly is more or less than human, though assuredly he is an enlightened and dedicated human; his total potentialities are subject to definite limits which Celia, for example, is outside. Alec Guinness, who played the role in the initial Edinburgh, Brighton, and New York runs of the play, said that he considers Reilly simply as a doctor. He pointed out that psychiatry is discussed much less openly in England than in the United States, and this fact perhaps partly accounts for the reticence of both Eliot and Guinness to discuss the problem in any detail.

Reilly is an enlightened mid-twentieth-century psychiatrist who recognizes the parallel insights of Eastern mysticism, Christian mysticism, and Jungian psychology and uses them as he is able in his efforts to help his patients. The compound of psychic content from Eastern and Christian religions seen in *The Cocktail Party* suggests Eliot's earlier poetic usage of such elements from as early as *The Waste Land* to the later *Four Quartets* and *The Family Reunion,* and it is also paralleled outside religious institutionalism in published writings and rituals of Freemasonry.

Reilly receives, of course, much indispensable aid from Julia and Alex, each of whom has particular and useful abilities for furthering their joint purposes. Reilly's insights into Celia's attitudes, for instance, come via Julia's sneak visit while Celia waits downstairs, not via divine or occult revelation.

In his excellent article, "Eliot's Comedy,"[4] W. K. Wimsatt questions Reilly's psychology, suggesting that the presumption of his speeches to Edward in Act I would have caused Edward to throw him out bodily; he also suggests that Reilly's blunt advice to Edward and Lavinia in Act II would not have been accepted. It seems to me, on the contrary, that Reilly convincingly exhibits throughout the play enough insight into the emotional workings of Edward and Lavinia to enable him to stretch them to the points at which they almost rebel (but not quite), thereby forcing them to learn things about themselves that they could not previously have recognized. At no point does he go beyond the judicious use of this awareness; he constantly uses their strong emotional reactions to get them to listen to more advice, criticism, and suggestions—to stay in his office, for instance, not only in spite of their indignation but because of it.

Though they are not made explicit in the play, a number of clues are given to the relationships among the three guardians. Since Reilly deals most directly with the three patients at their moments of enlightenment and decision, it seems natural to assume that he is the most authoritative member of the trio of guardians. In spite of his tipsy and raucous ballad at the first party, he attains considerable stature and dignity even in the first act, and still more during the interviews in Act II with Edward alone and then with Edward and Lavinia together; but Julia first impresses the audience as a boring old busybody and Alex seems less impressive than either of them. The audience is therefore considerably surprised when, after Edward and Lavinia have left Reilly's office Julia comes in and says, "Henry, get up. You can't be as tired as that. I shall wait in the next room,/And come back when she's gone." Though the audience does not know it yet, this is their first view of Julia without the sham and showmanship which characterized her in Act I.

After Celia comes in, makes her decision, and leaves, the audience is in for further startling revelations of Julia's character. Reilly says of Celia, "She will go far, that one." Julia replies, "Very far, I think./You do not need to tell me. I knew from the beginning." And slightly later, when he asks if Celia will be frightened by the appearance of projected spirits, Julia replies, "Henry, you simply do not understand innocence./She will be afraid of nothing; she will not even know/That there is anything there to be afraid of./She is too humble." Reilly says a little later, "When I express confidence in anything/You always raise doubts; when I am apprehensive/Then you see no reason for anything but confidence," to which Julia retorts, "That's one way in which I am so useful to you./You ought to be grateful."

Julia seems almost to have the advantage, but we must remember that the decision with regard to Edward and Lavinia which Reilly later questioned was his own: "I have taken a great risk."

The above quotations also suggest that the wisdom and abilities of both Reilly and Julia are incomplete—that only together are they capable of handling the more difficult problems. This complementarity of Reilly and Julia is seen in the one-eyed and spectacle references and is comically linked, by the ballad which Reilly sings, to his drinking of gin and water; and the humorous play on Reilly's drinking is continued in the second cocktail party in Act III, at which Julia drinks straight gin and Reilly only water. This bit of comedy reinforces the motif of complementarity seen in the spectacles episode and in the discussion in Reilly's office among the guardians—as does also their mutual ritual of libation and incantation.

Alex, like Julia, serves as an observer, arranger, contacter, and meddler in the lives of the patients. Like Julia again, he indulges in subterfuge, deception, and intrigue—whatever is necessary to motivate the proper responses in those whom the guardians are trying to help. Seeming at first a somewhat more bland character than either of his associates, he fits well in the cocktail-party society from which Reilly's clientele are drawn. It becomes evident in the third act that he also has administrative abilities, that he is a man of action as well as talk, and that his references throughout the play to his travels and affairs were not mere inventions. Alex's overtones are those of Eastern religion and organized social and political influence. He makes something out of nothing (a trick he learned in the East); he has connections everywhere; and, though at first he makes a much slighter impression than that of his two associates, he proves on close examination to be as integral a part of their operations as either.

It is a condition of the dramatic medium that the audience's knowledge of a character must be incomplete or at least subject to modification until the end of the play; Eliot's guardians, though, more than most dramatic characters, take on enigmatic auras because of the deception and the ambiguities in which they cloak their motives while furthering their purpose of helping the other characters. Part of the play's comedy lies in the light irony with which the true qualities of Julia and Alex are stated in Act I in such ways as to be discounted by the others (and by the audience). Shortly after the play begins, Celia says that Julia is such a good mimic; Peter adds that she never misses anything, and Alex adds, ". . . unless she wants to." Shortly after, Alex calls Julia "a mine of information," and Celia says "There isn't much that Julia doesn't know." Julia herself says to Edward, "I know what you're thinking!/I know you think I'm a silly old woman/ But I'm really very serious. Lavinia takes me seriously./I believe that's the reason why she went away—/So that I could make you talk." In a number of such remarks, Julia alludes to the true state of affairs between Edward and Lavinia, which he has not yet admitted. She repeatedly presses Edward on painful points which threaten to reveal his fabrication regarding Lavinia's sick aunt: "I understood these tough old women—/I'm one myself: I feel as if I knew/All about that aunt in Hampshire." And of course she does know all about Lavinia's absence and the reasons for it; and the old busybody that she seems to be is as much a fabrication as Lavinia's aunt. She presses the question, asking whether he has the address and telephone number so that she can drop in on Lavinia on her way to Cornwall; but then she mercifully changes the subject when she sees that Edward will not admit the truth.

Such direct hints as to the nature of the guardians are of course counterbalanced and robbed of credibility by the manner in which they are given, and also by the guardians' pretense that they do not know each other very well. Julia shows a fine sense of humor, as well as a fine disregard for veracity, when she returns for her umbrella and finds Edward drinking with the Unidentified Guest: "Now what are you two plotting?/How very lucky it was my umbrella,/And not Alexander's—*he's* so inquisitive!/But *I* never poke into other people's business." Julia, of course, does a considerable amount of poking into other people's business, seeming all the while a really unlikable old woman.

Alex also makes humorously symbolic statements of the real role of the guardians. Upon returning "to make sure that Edward gets dinner," he says, "I'm rather a famous cook./. . . that's my special gift—/Concocting a toothsome meal out of nothing./Any scraps you have will do. I learned that in the East." And at another level, the guardians are engaged in producing something psychically palatable from the scraps of the lives of Edward and Lavinia. (Celia has more than scraps to offer, perhaps.) While Edward and Peter are discussing Celia, the hypotenuse of one of the interlocking love triangles in the play, Alex significantly calls from the kitchen, "Edward, have you a double boiler?" Edward explains, a few speeches later, that there is no curry powder because Lavinia doesn't like it. Alex suggests the inadequacy of the materials with which the guardians must work in the Chamberlaynes' case and perhaps justifies the unspectacular success which Edward and Lavinia's treatment will bring when he says, "There goes another surprise, then. I must think./I didn't expect to find any mangoes,/But I *did* count upon curry powder." (The guardians have already found Lavinia evasive, but had still hoped that Edward would face Lavinia's departure more honestly than he has. Reilly makes it clear in the second act that their lack of honesty has forced him to go to the lengths seen in their confrontation in his office; and

earlier Julia, as already noted, has tried hard to provoke Edward
to drop his sham.)

Julia admits her subterfuges of the forgotten umbrella and
the lost spectacles when she leaves Edward and Lavinia in the
second scene of the first act. Edward asks, "Are you sure you
haven't left anything, Julia?" and she replies, "Left anything?
Oh, you mean my spectacles./No, they're here. Besides they're
no use to me./I'm not coming back again *this* evening."

Wimsatt questions the credibility of the guardians, asking,
"How can two such fatuous characters as Julia and Alex be
translated between the first and second acts into guardian
angels?" In the first place, the "fatuousness" of Julia and Alex
exists only at the literal level of their first-act speeches; and the
dramatic irony is reinforced by the overtones which an expert
actor will properly play into those lines; sheer fun is coupled
with deadly seriousness. Even at the literal level, their "fatuousness" is part and parcel of the deception which they employ to
conceal their real purposes. And, at that, much of their deception
consists in telling the exact truth in such ways that it is mistaken for meaningless or insincere party talk.

Further, no speech in the play—however inane or comic on
the surface—is without demonstrable connections to the central
themes of the play. The series of stories that never get told at
the first party may serve as an example. In the opening line of
the play, Alex's beginning of a story has been misinterpreted by
Julia. "There *were* no tigers," Alex insists, as if to answer the
critics who would read the play entirely in terms of Christian
symbols, ignoring Eliot's precautions to make the lines broader
than that in both basis and implications. (This line is effectively
repeated in the last act.) Julia's story of Lady Klootz and
the wedding cake leads into speculations on the nationality of
Lady Klootz, the family of Delia Verinder with its harmless
brother who could hear the cry of bats, and the dead parents
of Tony Vincewell—who was the product but not the solution
of their problems. All of these prefigure the confusion of
Lavinia's real aunt, who sent the eggs, with the prefabricated
aunt supplied by Edward to explain Lavinia's absence. They
also reflect the aborted relations between the characters of the
play and the tangled interrelations among them. And by prolong-
ing and finally defeating the listeners' expectations of hearing
the promised stories, they set the tone of frustration enveloping

the four non-guardians. They also parallel the Chamberlaynes' failure to come up with straight stories.

The relations among the guardians are subtly hinted throughout the play. Each of their actions and speeches in some way fills out the tenuous but tantalizing picture of their interworkings. They do not hesitate to interfere in other people's lives (though Reilly warns that it is a serious thing to do so and that forces are thus set in motion which cannot be altered). They use deception, harassing techniques, and the advantage given by their emotional insights in order to help their "patients." And finally, they emerge as a close-knit trio of enlightened humans who enjoy using their talents and awarenesses to help others become "similarly" enlightened—though each case is unique. Throughout the play they are surrounded by a considerable air of mystery.

Part III Problems of Act III

The most stringent and the most repeated criticisms of *The Cocktail Party* have been aimed at its third act, centering around Celia's death, Alex's description of it, and the supposed flatness and lowered interest of that act. Many critics have protested the "unnecessary violence" of Celia's death. W. K. Wimsatt, for example, says that her martyrdom, "aiming at something the opposite of tame, shoots both too far above the comic and too far wide of it, into the sensationally gruesome. . . . Alex . . . insists far too explicitly on the meaning of her name—a girl indeed 'enskied and sainted.' . . . and I can see no excuse for the manner of her death. . . . The failure of tact is only underscored by an elaborate introductory patter about monkeys, heathens, and Christian natives (part of the comedy). . . . Something more muted, nearly accidental, unheroic, was surely required. It could have been disagreeable enough."[4]

The same sort of objection was behind D. W. Harding's comment that "It is hard, for instance, to see a serious purpose in Reilly's account of his original intuition (expressed in an apparition) that Celia was destined to a violent death. It seems beside the point: the significance of her choice was unconnected with the variety of death to which she was on her way, and presumably Reilly's help would have been equally available to such a person whether she was to die from violence or disease or old age. It seems to be one of the incidents that fills out the stage play without being required by the dramatic theme."[5]

In his 1951 essay "Poetry and Drama," Eliot acknowledged such criticisms: "I am aware that the last act of my play only just escapes, if indeed it does escape, the accusation of being not a last act but an epilogue; and I am determined to do something different, if I can, in this respect."[6]

I am not certain what is wrong with a play's having an epilogue, even if Eliot's criticism were justified—which I do not believe it to be. Without the third act the play's psychic scheme would be incomplete and ambiguous; to omit it robs the audience of the evidence and materials on which must be based any valid estimate of the two previous acts: Are the "guardians" frauds? Only the altered behavior of Edward and Lavinia, as well as of the guardians, can tell us. Have Edward and Lavinia really put on proper costumes? Only the genuine warmth and consideration which they show each other in this so-called near-epilogue can tell us. Does Reilly's "sanatorium" meet Celia's needs? Alex tells us in Act III. And beyond these essential matters, much of the rounding-out of the play's excellent comedy is accomplished in this final act with its echoes of acts I and II, its parallels, extensions, and developments of the imagery and the humor of the earlier acts.

Nonetheless, the primary function of the third act is not the communication of reports and information:

> ALEX: We have just drawn up an interim report.
> EDWARD: Will it be made public?
> ALEX: It cannot be, at present:
>   There are too many international complications.
>   Eventually, there may be an official publication.

So we must presently be satisfied with the allegory of the monkeys who eat crops, Christians who eat monkeys, and heathens who eat Christians who have eaten monkeys.

The important thing in Act III, to repeat, is not ideas, but rather the opportunity for the auditor himself to observe the changed quality of behavior—the changed psychic focus—of the various characters, so that he can leave the theatre with a well-grounded and satisfactory estimate of what has been accomplished in the play.

Readers who find the felicity of Edward and Lavinia too tame, their domesticity and goodness unpalatable on the stage, must either have failed to follow the central development of the second act or must simply be uninterested in the matters with which it deals. Moreover, it seems necessary that Celia's death be as violent and shocking as it is in order that we may see what is truly significant in that death. In Reilly's unshocked and even pleased reaction to the account, which Lavinia makes certain that we shall not overlook, we can see—having now been given the basis for trust in his diagnosis and his comments—that shock is not the proper reaction: that the manner of Celia's death, the realistic and accidental details, do not matter.

What does matter, as Krishna said to Arjuna on the battle-field in the *Bhagavad-Gita*, is the psychic focus at the hour of death—"And the time of death is every moment"; "every moment is a new beginning"; "Oh, I'm glad. It's begun." What mattered was the altered quality of Celia's experience, the essential change in her attitudes, expectations, and concerns which had ensued. From the fact that all of the characters except Peter Quilpe are capable of humor, of looking at the right side of the coin, even in the context of such topics as Celia's martyrdom, we receive something more than just entertainment and clarification of the dramatic scheme: The play, and the audience, are brought back to the familiar world where we started in Act I. Lavinia's final remark, "Oh, I'm glad. It's begun," brings the auditor back to the concrete sidewalk in front of the theatre with the therapeutically right echo in his ears and with a sufficiently non-rational orientation to satisfy the most angry of young men.

Richard Lonkin wrote that in *The Cocktail Party*, as in *Four Quartets* and *Notes Toward the Definition of Culture*, Eliot "has used all the resources of his wide and long experience to make simple and understandable for us important things which no other living writer cares or dares to write about." In this play, Eliot has made more explicit than might reasonably have been hoped the Aristotelian-Dantean psychic scheme that has been at the center of his prose, his poems, and his plays with surprisingly little change since the days of *Prufrock*.

II The Confidential Clerk

Like its predecessors, Eliot's play *The Confidential Clerk* (1954) was noticeably influenced by classical drama. But in this case, for the first time, the reader is strongly reminded of the heavily plotted Roman comedies which, like this play, took many cues from the *Ion* of Euripides. There are clear and detailed parallels between Eliot's and Euripides' play.[7] In addition to the lost children, the searching parents, and the mistaken identities, the casts of characters and the basic plots are similar. As Ion's father was Apollo, the god of poetry and music, Colby Simpkins' dead father was an organist and his real father turns out to be God, with the confidential clerk Eggerson, "the only developed Christian in the play," standing-in as interim father until Colby can find his true vocation.

Briefly, the plot is as follows: Sir Claude and Lady Elizabeth Mulhammer had each, about twenty-five years before the play begins, had a child born out of wedlock—at least Sir Claude thought he had, though it turns out at the end that the girl who was to bear his child died without giving birth (he was off in Canada for a year or so) and the baby (Colby) that he thought was his was really the son of her widowed and destitute sister, Mrs. Guzzard. Lady Elizabeth's child had been put out to nurse by her fiance, and, when he was killed in Africa by a rhinoceros, his family denied all responsibility for the child; and the embarrassed Elizabeth, unable to press inquiries, failed in her efforts to locate her baby.

As the play opens, Sir Claude has brought Colby, whom he has supported all these years, into his household as a replacement for his retiring confidential clerk, Mr. Eggerson. He hopes that Lady Elizabeth, due home from abroad, will learn to accept Colby as one of the family, after which he may tell her that Colby is his illegitimate son. She accepts Colby immediately and convinces herself that he is her lost baby grown up. Colby, meanwhile, is not sure that he has found his proper vocation as a confidential clerk, not having fully given up his former aspirations to become an organist. Sir Claude has also an acknowledged illegitimate daughter, Lucasta Angel, who is engaged to Mr. Barnabas Kaghan, a promising young businessman. In Act III Eggerson presides over a meeting of all the principals in which it is learned through Mrs. Guzzard that Colby is her own son, that Sir Claude never had a son, and that Barnabas Kaghan is Lady Elizabeth's son (probably). Learning that his real father was a moderately successful musician, Colby decides to follow his inner promptings to become a church organist. Under the protection of Eggerson, the real confidential clerk, he leaves the household of the Mulhammers for a new life of his own. Lucasta and Barnaby will be married, and Sir Claude and Lady Elizabeth will have their son and daughter. Mrs. Guzzard will have nobody.

The confusions of the plot are compounded in the first two

acts, and the third act has a great deal of unraveling to accomplish. We feel in reading it that this play needs to be seen and not just read before it can be criticized confidently. More than any of Eliot's earlier plays, it seems to have verve and vigor realizable only on the stage, though it would place heavy demands on the skills of the director and the players. But in reading it, we recognize that Eliot has again dealt with a number of themes found in his earlier works, especially in *The Cocktail Party*: themes of the interrelatedness of lives, the necessity of making decisions and accepting their consequences, the importance of finding one's vocation, the ease and seriousness of self-deception, the dangers of trying to manage other people's lives, and the existence of a tougher self that must be painfully discovered if one is to find fulfillment.

Most of the play's characters echo others in the author's previous plays and poems: Colby is noticeably related to Thomas, Harry, and Celia; and, like them, he can be traced to Prufrock, Gerontion, and the protagonists of *The Waste Land* and *Ash-Wednesday*. Sir Claude Mulhammer, Colby's would-be father, shares with Amy of *The Family Reunion* the shattering of plans and the loss of a son. Eggerson, the confidential clerk, echoes some aspects of Sir Henry Harcourt-Reilly in *The Cocktail Party*; and of course Sir Claude and Lady Elizabeth must, like Edward and Lavinia, settle for what they have and "make the best of a bad job," which will be altered in the doing, as can already be seen in the new sympathy for each other displayed in Act III of each of the two plays.

Eliot's concern to approach the language and rhythms of speech seems to have been marvelously achieved in this play. In "Poetry and Drama" he wrote that when writing *The Cocktail Party* he had "laid down for myself the ascetic rule to avoid poetry which could not stand the test of strict dramatic utility." (See note 6.) In reading *The Confidential Clerk* we are even less aware of reading poetry, and yet there is excellent poetry in both of the plays.

If *The Cocktail Party* was distinguished by Eliot's placing great emphasis for the first time on more humble characters not destined to be saints, the same emphasis is even stronger in *The Confidential Clerk*. It is true, as D. E. Jones points out, that B. Kaghan in the play calls Colby the sort of person who might chuck it all and go off to a desert island, but that is the closest we come to a Harry or a Celia in this milder potential church-organist and perhaps eventual cleric. In this play, as in *The Cocktail Party*, every character is involved in tracing out his proper identity and inheritance, and several of them are concerned with resolving the life of two worlds in neither of which they feel at home. All of them, except Colby, are intent on finding satisfactory and close relationship with other characters in the play; only Colby wants to be free of others, and the resolution of Act III gives all of them what they want, though we may suspect that a stronger relationship will develop between Colby and the Eggersons than he then intends.

Throughout the play may be found various echoes of the *Bhagavad-Gita*. Eggerson's almost paradoxical admixture of deference and of sure control may prove less puzzling if we remember that Krishna was incarnated as the charioteer and advisor of Arjuna, a parallel that is reinforced by various details in *The Confidential Clerk*. Echoes from the *Bhagavad-Gita* also make Lady Elizabeth's meanderings in mysticism seem less flighty and incoherent, and the theme of playing one's own proper role and not someone else's is of course central to that religious classic so admired by Eliot and importantly used in a number of his works.

In this respect, Sir Claude raises the question of whether or not one can have a vocation to be a second-class artist; and that is what Colby at the end decides that he has, but the fact that it is his real heritage contents him. And Sir Claude comes to suspect that he was wrong to deny his own real vocation as a second-class potter for his role as a successful but not great financier. As with Celia, it is a larger dose of honesty than any other character in the play possesses that makes Colby unable to accept the sort of compromise that Sir Claude has lived with for many years, that makes Colby refuse both the make-believe of Lady Elizabeth's world and the alternatives offered him by Sir Claude. Only Eggerson sees this and avoids the error of trying to make Colby be what he is not. And thus it is only Eggerson to whom Colby will listen at the end of the play.

Already in *The Cocktail Party* Eliot had felt real compassion and respect for every character. In *The Confidential Clerk* the human dignity of each character is even more marked. Even Mrs. Guzzard is given more compelling claims on our understanding and sympathy than a number of earlier characters in Eliot's plays. (Even the fairy-like wish-granting which seems to stylize her big scene for the sake of farce is not without its serious and symbolic undertones.) Finally, as she points out, each of the characters has been allowed to choose a wish and to have it granted; but, when she and Sir Claude made their choices twenty-five years previously, they had failed to realize that there would be a time limit for them. At the play's end the audience's sympathy with her is reestablished when it is seen that she alone of all the characters has gotten nothing from the climactic recognition scene—she has, in fact, lost what little she had.

As Grover Smith points out, there is some question of the accuracy of the "facts" that she reveals. I believe, however, that whether they are authentic or not makes very little difference to the major themes of the play, though it does add force to the farce when we understand that they are doubtful.

III The Elder Statesman

Though each of Eliot's plays has been markedly different in one or more ways from its predecessors, a surprising continuity of theme accompanies the innovations of technique. In *The Elder Statesman* may be found most of the main themes already discussed in connection with the earlier plays.[8] However, it deals with love between persons more fully and more warmly than any of the previous works—*Marina* being the only near-exception.

Just as *Little Gidding* marked the ultimate development in directions long integral to Eliot's poems, *The Elder Statesman* seems a definitive statement concluding lines of development seen in all of the earlier plays. It seems thus highly appropriate that this play should take as a model *Oedipus at Colonus*, the climactic work of Sophocles' dramatic career.

In Act I of *The Elder Statesman* we see first the realization of Lord Claverton's daughter Monica and Charles Hemington that they love each other and want to marry when it becomes possible for them to do so without depriving Lord Claverton of the company and care that he needs. Next we meet the unsavory Federico Gomez, formerly Lord Claverton's classmate Fred Culverwell and then a convicted forger. Having made his fortune in Central America, Gomez has come back and intends to force his company on Claverton by threatening to tell a story of a youthful escapade in which their car ran over a man on the road.

Act II is set in Badgley Court, a convalescent home where Lord Claverton, accompanied by Monica, hopes to find rest and quiet. Instead, he finds the mistakes of his youth turning up in the persons of Mrs. Carghill, who once sued him for breach of promise, and Gomez. Also his son Michael, repeating his own earlier failings, gives him cause to worry.

Act III, though it produces complications and discomforts when Gomez and Mrs. Carghill vent their old resentments against Lord Claverton by getting his son Michael to leave for Central America with Gomez, brings also a satisfactory conclusion to Monica's father. He confesses to Monica and Charles the nature of his ghosts, and he discovers the real self behind the sham roles he has played all his life. He also blesses their love and offers the prediction that they will be free of the self-deceptions that have wasted much of his life. In the end, his love for his children and Monica's love for him enable him to die happy.

As throughout Eliot's works, we find in this play many lines that echo and clarify earlier ones. Colby, for example, told Lucasta in *The Confidential Clerk* that if anyone were to share his private world, "it can't be done by issuing invitations:/They would just have to come. And I should not see them coming./I should not hear the opening of the gate./They would simply . . . be there suddenly,/Unexpectedly. Walking down an alley/I should become aware of someone walking with me." And in *The Elder Statesman* Monica says of the first satisfying human love in all of Eliot's plays, "How did this come, Charles? It crept so softly/On silent feet, and stood behind my back/Quietly, a long time, a long long time/Before I felt its presence."

Lord Claverton uses railway imagery similar to that of the *Four Quartets* and ghost imagery suggesting that of *Little Gidding*. He says, "They won't want my ghost/Walking in the City or sitting in the Lords./And I, who recognise myself as a ghost/Shan't want to be seen there." The drink-pouring of Gomez echoes that of Sir Henry Harcourt-Reilly. And Lord Claverton's line "What is this self inside us, this silent observer,/Severe and speechless critic, who can terrorise us/And urge us on to futile activity,/And in the end, judge us still more severely/For the errors into which his own reproaches drove us" suggests the "tougher self" speech of Edward in *The Cocktail Party*.

Mrs. Carghill's "There were the three of us—Effie, Maudie, and me./That day we spent on the river—I've never forgotten it—/The turning point of all my life!" suggests the three Thames-daughters of *The Waste Land,* perhaps, and her " 'That man is hollow' " suggests of course *The Hollow Men.* When Michael says of his father's influence, "And what satisfaction, I wonder, will it give you/In the grave? If you are still conscious after death,/I bet it will be a surprised state of consciousness./Poor ghost! reckoning up its profit and loss/And wondering why it bothered about such trifles," we are reminded of the surprised soul after death in Dante and in *Animula,* of Reilly's vision of Celia in *The Cocktail Party,* and of the profit and loss of Phlebas the Phoenician in *Dans le restaurant* and *The Waste Land.* And other echoes too (as in *Burnt Norton*) inhabit this garden.

What is new in this play, as we said, is the emphasis on love, also paralleled in *Oedipus at Colonus,* in which Oedipus says, "My children, to-day your father leaves you. This is the end of all that was I, and the end of your long task of caring for me. I know how hard it was. Yet it was made lighter by one word— love. I loved you as no one else had ever done. Now you must live on without me."[9] The echoes of *Oedipus at Colonus* are many and detailed, but they are not essential to an understanding of *The Elder Statesman.* Very few details have been taken over from Sophocles without being wholly integrated into the dramatic structure. This represents an improvement over especially *The Family Reunion,* in which the Eumenides obtruded seriously between the audience and the play, and over *The Cocktail Party,* in which Sir Henry's raucous behavior in drinking seemed out of character until linked with Heracles' exuberant display in Euripides' *Alcestis.* It is, of course, the grove of those same Eumenides that pursued Harry in which Oedipus takes refuge and dies, but in *The Elder Statesman* they are replaced by the live ghosts from Lord Claverton's past, Freddie Culverwell and Maisie Montjoy—and by Dick Ferry, his own earlier ghost.

Again we suspect that this play requires a great deal of the actors who perform it but that, given a highly skilled stage presentation, it could be extremely effective.

Like *The Confidential Clerk, The Elder Statesman* is likely to appeal most to mature adults, and especially to parents; it may seem too tame and too happy to the young reader who has deeply empathized with the frustrations of those of Eliot's tortured protagonists still farther from felicity than the sixty-year-old Lord Claverton and less understood and loved than Monica and Charles are by each other. The play is sure to gain

in impressiveness as such a reader gets farther from and understands better some of his own mistakes—and especially after he
has become involved in the search for ways of helping his
children to avoid repeating his own errors. Its concern with the
ways in which a parent's well-intended hedging against any
admission of his greatest weaknesses or failings can ensure the
same failings in children, and on the ways in which the parent's
concern to project his own ambitions or desires makes the child
feel unloved can hardly fail to engage the interest of parents.
As in *The Family Reunion* and in *The Confidential Clerk*, the
nature and history of the family curse is a central concern
of this play. It is fitting that Eliot's Greek model involved
Oedipus, a man who, however unwittingly, succumbed to the
curse on his family but salvaged a measure of grace at the end,
even though he did not succeed in ending the curse.

The effect of *The Elder Statesman*, especially when considered in conjunction with all of Eliot's other works, is one of
unexpected and unearned grace, of liberation and restoration
through the healing power of a love—a human love that had
seemed inaccessible throughout most of the author's career.

The reader cannot doubt the sincerity and the accuracy of
the dedicatory poem, which points to such a love in the author's
second marriage as is seen in the play. *The Elder Statesman*
is likely to command more and more admiration, and to rival
Murder in the Cathedral and *The Cocktail Party* as Eliot's
masterpiece of the theatre.

CHAPTER 9

Conclusion

IN DISCUSSING the differences between English and American poetry and the question whether Auden should be considered English or American, Eliot said that whichever Auden is, he himself must be the other.[1] As shown in Chapter 1, the significant soil from which Eliot and his poetry sprang was that of St. Louis and New England, but the imagery and echoes from both of these settings have been given a more universal quality and combined with the imagery of England, his adopted country, and of Paris. In such a poem as *The Dry Salvages* the Mississippi has become very similar to Conrad's Congo or Thames and has shared its themes with Eliot's Thames.

But Eliot's roots go back not just to eighteenth-century New England or seventeenth-century East Coker; they go back to the whole of the Western literary culture—especially to its beginnings in Greece, to Dante, and to the Elizabethans—and also to the works of Eastern philosophy that have occupied his attention since his student days in the first decade of the twentieth century.

Eliot spoke in his "A Talk on Dante" of the poet to whom one grows up over a lifetime, from whom one can get enough on first reading to make the poetry rewarding, but from whom one gets more and more as time goes on. Certainly Eliot is this kind of poet himself. Much of his poetry becomes simplest and most resonant after one reads widely in Western literature. Most of his borrowings, however, need not be returned to their original contexts in order to follow his uses of them; usually the new context supplies quite adequate clues to the significance and function in Eliot's own poem. But the reader who familiarizes himself with the works on which Eliot draws and to which he alludes will find Eliot's poems richer and more subtle, though paradoxically simpler. He will also find his time well spent: For one thing, Eliot will not steer him to literature not worth reading in and for itself; for another, the close comparison of a number of Eliot's borrowings in both their old and new contexts will teach the reader much about Eliot's artistic practice and about the nature and functioning of literary sensibility. He will discover that Eliot always transmutes the borrowing into a new and different unity and that in the process the borrowed words often gain impressiveness and precision. And while enabling himself to read Eliot more effectively, he will broaden and deepen his awareness of our literary and philosophical heritage.

The wedding of Christianity to the classical tradition, which achieves its highest literary expression in Dante's works, is found to be a basic groundwork, a constant vantage point throughout Eliot's poems and plays. Dante's theology and theory of the soul give eternal significance to individual lives and unique events. They emphasize the tragic import of a ruined life, whether that of a Dantean shade in hell or one of Eliot's wastelanders.

The influence of Dante is crucial to the interpretation of even the earliest of Eliot's poems, and it is chiefly through overlooking that influence and its meanings that many critics have been able to ignore the religious content and intent of those early poems that largely avoided the use—or rather the exclusive use—of Christian symbols. We need not agree with Eliot's theology, any more than with Dante's, to be moved by his poetry. Because his poems express authentic states growing out of belief, we can admire the expression of the state even if we reject the belief; but, of course, the reader who accepts the belief will derive additional enjoyment from the reading.

Eliot's insistence that it is the poetry and not the life of the poet in which we are interested is clarified by his saying of Dante that it was not because his experiences happened to him, Dante, but because they had meaning in themselves that certain of them were incorporated into his poems. In Eliot's works, similarly, it is not the biographical fact, the experience, that is significant; it is the meaning that emerges later and is the reason for including the experience in the poetry—the happiness or agony or desire, or the love. The distinction between what might have been and what has been becomes unimportant if the poem is successful, and it is uninteresting if not. What we need to understand is not the writer's history but the outlooks and orientations behind his works—the logic of sensibility built into them.

Nevertheless we may legitimately be concerned with biography insofar as it sheds light on the works themselves and on the wholly or partially realized intentions behind them. Eliot's removal to England, for example, seems to have introduced into his art elements unlikely for a wholly American or a wholly English poet—to have expanded his cultural consciousness through mutual qualifyings of two related but divergent social and traditional contexts.

Eliot's formal adoption of Anglican orthodoxy (and of British citizenship) in 1927 was echoed in his poetic works of the same period, in the more overtly Christian orientation, themes, and imagery of *Ash-Wednesday, The Rock,* and *Murder in the Cathedral.* The same period brought the turning of interest toward the writing of verse drama; and, though the first plays, *Sweeney Agonistes, The Rock,* and *Murder in the Cathedral,* were followed by the *Four Quartets*—perhaps the greatest of his poems—Eliot's attention turned more and more exclusively toward the theatre. The doctrines of social responsibility enunciated in such works as *The Idea of a Christian Society* and *Notes Towards the Definition of Culture* clarify the motives for turning to this more public art form. The plays, like the poems, continued to draw on the whole of the literary tradition and especially on the Greek dramatists, bringing to an ever-wider audience some of the same basic themes and perceptions emphasized as early as *Prufrock.*

Among Eliot's major contributions to our tradition are his labors to re-establish the popularity of verse drama and his finding of verse forms appropriate to the speech of the twentieth-century world. Both in his poetic practice and in his critical pronouncements these matters have received constant emphasis. Throughout his career Eliot has emphasized the responsibilities of the poet not only to entertain, but to expand the awareness of his reader and to assist him in man's perpetual struggle to rediscover the best that has been revealed and lost again and again by others before him. The search for the deeper identity, the tougher self, requiring the painful shedding of illusions and the recognition of the falseness of projections of what one wants to see, is found from *Prufrock* to *The Elder Statesman*—from the involved constriction of Prufrock to the free and open simplicity of Lord Claverton's final speeches and of Monica's love for Charles.

In *The Use of Poetry and the Use of Criticism* (1933), Eliot wrote:

Every poet would like, I fancy, to be able to think that he had some direct social utility. By this, as I hope I have already made clear, I do not mean that he should meddle with the tasks of the theologian, the preacher, the economist, the sociologist or anybody else; that he should do anything but write poetry, poetry not defined in terms of something else. He would like to be something of a popular entertainer, and be able to think his own thoughts behind a tragic or a comic mask. He would like to convey the pleasures of poetry, not only to a larger audience, but to larger groups of people collectively; and the theatre is the best place in which to do it. There might, one fancies, be some fulfillment in exciting this communal pleasure, to give an immediate compensation for the pains of turning blood into ink. As things are, and as fundamentally they must always be, poetry is not a career, but a mug's game. No honest poet can ever feel quite sure of the permanent value of what he has written: he may have wasted his time and messed up his life for nothing. All the better, then, if he could have at least the satisfaction of having a part to play in society as worthy as that of the music-hall comedian.[2]

Within ten years Eliot's poetry was to be devoted almost wholly to the theatre, and surely the successes that he has enjoyed there and the recognition accorded his poetry might have removed some of the doubts expressed. I am sure many readers must regret that after the *Four Quartets* Eliot turned almost exclusively to the theatre, and yet the plays impress us more and more at each rereading, as many plays do not.

The uncertainty of the artist's future was again referred to when in 1953 Eliot wrote that he did not look forward with joy to literary oblivion nor to the time when his works might be read only by several graduate students enrolled in "Middle Anglo-American 42 B."[3]

Surveying the whole body of writings from *Prufrock* to *The Elder Statesman*, we are struck by the continuity of subject matter and aims no less than by the flexibility and innovation of techniques visible in any one of the decades since 1911. Even should our language be replaced—like those of Sophocles and Lucretius, of Arnaut Daniel and even, to some extent, of Shakespeare—the great works of our time will still be read, loved, and translated; and there seems to be no danger that Eliot's will not be among them. Even the dead weight of endless criticism is hardly likely to obscure the beauties and merits of his best works.

As early as 1932, Hugh Ross Williamson could write "It is no exaggeration to say that there is no young poet at present writing who does not owe something to T. S. Eliot."[4] Despite his detractors, Eliot since then has come to be recognized as the elder statesman of English letters. (Donald Gallup's 1953 bibliography already listed translations of his works into twenty-two languages.) Certainly the pleasures of poetry are various. Not all readers' minds operate in the same ways, nor, as Eliot has said, do those of all poets. Though the range of purposes and subjects in Eliot's works is narrower than those undertaken by some authors, within that range it is unlikely that his achievements will be surpassed. He has done more than any other writer to explore and expand the possibilities of twentieth-century poetry in English.

Notes and References

Chapter One

1. "The Influence of Landscape upon the Poet," *Daedalus* (Spring, 1960), p. 422.

2. *American Literature and the American Language*, Washington University Studies, New Series, Language and Literature, No. 23 (St. Louis, 1953), pp. 4-5.

3. *American Literature and the American Language*, p. 19.

4. *The Use of Poetry and the Use of Criticism: Studies in the Relation of Criticism to Poetry in England* (London, 1937), p. 33.

5. *American Literature and the American Language*, p. 5.

6. For complete bibliographical information on all of Eliot's publications to 1952, the reader should see Donald Gallup, *T. S. Eliot: A Bibliography* (New York, 1953).

7. Quoted in Kristian Smidt, *Poetry and Belief in the Work of T. S. Eliot*, rev. ed. (New York, 1961), p. 7. Chapter I of Smidt, "Background and Influences," is an excellent introduction to Eliot's early years.

8. *The Sacred Wood: Essays on Poetry and Criticism* (New York, 1960), p. 5.

9. Printed as "A Talk on Dante," *Kenyon Review*, XIV (Spring 1952), 179-80. Compare this with the "Unreal City" sections of *The Waste Land* and with the "familiar compound ghost" section of *Little Gidding*. Much has been written on the influences of French poets on Eliot's early poems; fine brief accounts may be found in Smidt, cited above, and Hugh Kenner, *The Invisible Poet: T. S. Eliot* (New York, 1959).

10. Unless otherwise noted, all quotations from Eliot's poems and plays are taken from *The Complete Poems and Plays, 1909-1950* (New York, 1952).

11. From *Collected Poems 1909-1962* by T. S. Eliot, copyright, 1936, by Harcourt, Brace & World, Inc.; Faber & Faber Ltd.; (c) 1963, 1964, by T. S. Eliot. Reprinted by permission of the publishers.

12. Smidt, p. 20.

13. *Ibid.*, p. 21.

14. Ezra Pound, *Letters, 1907-1941*, ed. D. D. Paige (New York, 1950), p. 40.

15. *Ibid.*, p. 30.

16. *Ibid.*, p. 50.

17. These five poems were included: *The Love Song of J. Alfred Prufrock, Portrait of a Lady, The Boston Evening Transcript, Hysteria,* and *Miss Helen Slingsby [Aunt Helen].*

18. *Dante* (London, 1929).

19. Quoted in Kenner, p. 96.

20. F. O. Matthiessen, *The Achievement of T. S. Eliot: An Essay on the Nature of Poetry,* 3rd ed. (New York, 1959), p. xxi.

21. Reprinted in *The Little Review Anthology,* ed. Margaret Anderson (New York, 1953), p. 103.

22. *Ibid.,* pp. 103-4.

23. *Ibid.,* p. 108.

24. Quoted in "T. S. Eliot," *Ezra Pound,* ed. Peter Russell (London, 1950), p. 33.

Chapter Two

1. *The Sacred Wood* (New York, 1960), p. 164.

2. "Dante," *Selected Essays of T. S. Eliot,* new ed. (New York, 1950), p. 226.

3. *Ibid.,* pp. 236-37.

4. "Dante," pp. 220-21.

5. Matthiessen, p. 76.

6. See Leonard Unger, "Fusion and Experience," *The Man in the Name* (Minneapolis, 1956).

7. I have consistently used the excellent notes and occasionally quoted from the Dorothy L. Sayers translation of Dante's *The Divine Comedy* in the Penguin Classics, the following volumes: *I: Hell* (Baltimore, 1951); *II: Purgatory* (1955); and *III: Paradise,* trans. completed by Barbara Reynolds (1962). In general, however, I have followed Eliot's suggestion and used the bilingual Temple Classics edition of the following volumes: *The Inferno of Dante Alighieri* (London, 1946); *The Purgatorio of Dante Alighieri;* and *The Paradiso of Dante Alighieri.* For consistency throughout the text, I have also followed Eliot's example by referring to the whole work as *Divine Comedy* and the parts as *Inferno, Purgatorio,* and *Paradiso.*

This passage is from the Penguin Classics *Purgatory,* p. 265.

8. Temple Classics, *Purgatorio,* p. 217.

9. *Ibid.*

10. For example, in *A General Introduction to Psychoanalysis,* trans. Joan Riviere (New York, 1961), p. 112, Freud says, "I have already taken the liberty of pointing out to you that there is within you a deeply rooted belief in psychic freedom and choice, that this belief is quite unscientific, and that it must give ground before the claims of a determinism which governs even mental life."

11. This is also the theory expressed in William James, "Will," *Psychology* (Cleveland, 1948), Chapter 26.

12. Temple Classics, *Purgatorio,* pp. 219, 221.

13. See Aristotle's *Metaphysics,* 1070a, and *De anima.*

Chapter Three

1. Elizabeth Drew, *T. S. Eliot: The Design of His Poetry* (New York, 1949), pp. 40-41.

2. Kenner says that this poem "is deliberately involved in Eliot's besetting vice, a never wholly penetrable ambiguity about what is supposed to be happening" (p. 92). This charge contrasts with the tenor of most of Mr. Kenner's book.

3. Matthiessen, p. 59.

Chapter Four

1. Quoted in Matthiessen, p. 106.

2. "One of Lawrence's Letters," quoted in Matthiessen, p. 89.

3. Unpublished lecture on "English Letterwriters," New Haven, Connecticut, 1933; quoted in Matthiessen, p. 90.

4. G. S. Fraser, *The Modern Writer and His World* (London, 1953), p. 209.

5. Jessie L. Weston, *From Ritual to Romance* (New York, 1957), p. 126.

6. *Ibid.*, p. 76.

7. F. R. Leavis, *New Bearings in English Poetry* (London, 1954), pp. 95-96.

8. Charles Williams, *The Greater Trumps* (London, 1932).

9. "Religion and Literature," *Selected Essays.*

10. Philo M. Buck, *Directions in Contemporary Literature* (New York, 1942), pp. 275-77.

11. "Dante," *Selected Essays*, p. 217.

12. "Buddha's Fire Sermon" is here quoted from *The Sacred Book of the East,* trans. F. Max Muller, XIII (Oxford, 1881), 134-35. (Mahavagga, I, 21, i-iv.):

1. And the Blessed One, after having dwelt at Uruvela as long as he thought fit, went forth to Gayasisa, accompanied by a great number of Bhikkhus, by one thousand Bhikkhus who all had been Gatilas before. There near Gaya, at Gayasisa, the Blessed One dwelt together with those thousand Bhikkhus.

2. There the Blessed One thus addressed the Bhikkhus: "Everything, O Bhikkhus, is burning. And how, O Bhikkhus, is everything burning?

"The eye, O Bhikkhus, is burning; visible things are burning; the mental impressions based on the eye are burning; the contact of the eye (with visible things) is burning; the sensation produced by the contact of the eye (with visible things), be it pleasant, be it painful, be it neither pleasant nor painful, that also is burning. With what fire is it burning? I declare unto you that it is burning with the fire of lust, with the fire of anger, with the fire of ignorance; it is burning with (the anxieties of) birth, decay, death, grief, lamentation, suffering, dejection, and despair.

3. "The ear is burning, sounds are burning, &c. . . . The nose is burning, odours are burning, &c. . . . The tongue is burning, tastes are burning, &c. . . . The body is burning, objects of contact are burning, &c. . . . The mind is burning, thoughts are burning, &c. . . . (Author's note: Here the same exposition which has been given relating to the eye, its objects, the sensations produced by its contact with objects, &c., is repeated with reference to the ear and the other organs of sense.)

4. "Considering this, O Bhikkhus, a disciple learned (in the scriptures), walking in the Noble Path, becomes weary of the eye, weary of visible things, weary of the mental impressions based on the eye, weary of the contact of the eye (with visible things), weary also of the sensation produced by the contact of the eye (with visible things), be it pleasant, be it painful, be it neither pleasant nor painful. He becomes weary of the ear (&c. . . ., down to . . . thoughts). Becoming weary of all that, he divests himself of passion; by absence of passion he is made free; when he is free, he becomes aware that he is free; and he realises that re-birth is exhausted; that holiness is completed; that duty is fulfilled; and that there is no further return to this world."

When this exposition was propounded, the minds of those thousand Bhikkhus became free from attachment to the world, and were released from the Asavas.

———————————

Here ends the sermon on "The Burning."

———————————

End of the third Bhanavara concerning
the Wonders done at Uruvela.

13. *Thirteen Upanishads,* trans. Robert Ernest Hume (London, 1921), p. 150.

14. See Unger, "Laforgue, Conrad, and Eliot," *The Man in the Name,* pp. 234-37.

15. Thomas Kyd, *The Spanish Tragedy* in *Elizabethan and Stuart Plays,* ed. Charles Read Baskervill, *et al.* (New York, 1934), Act IV, Scene 1. I have used Eliot's spelling of Hieronymo throughout.

Chapter Five

1. D. E. S. Maxwell, *The Poetry of T. S. Eliot* (New York, 1961).

2. "Dante," *Selected Essays,* p. 235.

3. "A Dialogue on Dramatic Poetry," *Selected Essays,* pp. 22-40.

Notes and References

Carl Wooton, in his *Arizona Quarterly* (Spring, 1961) article "The Mass: Ash-Wednesday's Objective Correlative," says that the structure of the Mass is "loosely imposed on the whole poem." His interpretation, though suggestive as to major parallels, is marred by failure to recognize the important Dantean elements and by attempts to relate both the penitent and the celebrant-priest to the poem's protagonist.

4. *Vita Nuova*, trans. D. G. Rossetti, Temple Classics (London, 1930), p. 138.

5. Temple Classics, *Purgatorio*, p. 301.

6. An excellent, relevant book on the meaning of Beatrice here is Charles Williams' *The Figure of Beatrice* (New York, 1961).

7. Dorothy L. Sayers in her note to Canto XXIV, Penguin Classics, *Purgatory*.

8. Temple Classics, *Paradiso*, p. 39.

9. Penguin Classics, *Hell*, p. 75.

10. The bone, bird, and juniper tree imagery of Part II is also found in Jakob Grimm's fairy tale *The Juniper Tree*. Leonard Unger comments on this in *T. S. Eliot: A Selected Critique* (New York, 1948), pp. 357-58.

11. Suggested by Sister Mary Cleophas in her "*Ash-Wednesday*: the *Purgatorio* in a Modern Mode," *Comparative Literature*, XI (Fall 1959), 329-39.

12. C. S. Lewis, *The Allegory of Love: A Study in Medieval Tradition* (New York, 1958), p. 5.

13. "Dante," *Selected Essays*, p. 222.

14. Penguin Classics, *Purgatory*, p. 348.

15. Temple Classics, *Purgatorio*, p. 397.

16. Quoted in Unger, *The Man in the Name*, p. 162.

17. Quoted in Giorgio de Santillana, *The Origins of Scientific Thought* (New York, 1961), p. 44.

18. "Lancelot Andrewes," *Selected Essays*, p. 307.

19. These are reprinted as the appendix in Maxwell.

20. George Williamson, *A Reader's Guide to T. S. Eliot* (New York, 1957), p. 201.

Chater Six

1. This essay is reprinted in *Selected Essays*, where it can be readily consulted by readers who want to pursue these varying views, too often indiscriminately quoted as Eliot's own.

2. "A Dialogue on Dramatic Poetry," *Selected Essays*, p. 33.

3. *The Rock* (London, 1934), pp. 47-48.

4. David E. Jones, *The Plays of T. S. Eliot* (Toronto, 1960), p. 47.

5. *The Rock*, pp. 50-51.

6. *Ibid.*, p. 39.

7. "The Possibility of a Poetic Drama," *The Sacred Wood*, p. 70.

8. "The Three Voices of Poetry," *On Poetry and Poets* (New York, 1957), p. 96. For the conditions under which Eliot's early plays were written and the lessons that Eliot drew from them, the reader should consult besides that essay, "Poetry and Drama" in *On Poetry and Poets* and E. Martin Browne's "The Dramatic Verse of T. S. Eliot" in *T. S. Eliot: A Symposium*, ed. Richard March and M. J. Tambimuttu (Chicago, 1949).

9. "The Three Voices of Poetry," pp. 98-99.

10. Several excellent critiques of this play are available, but none better than that of Francis Fergusson in his *The Idea of a Theatre* (Princeton, 1949), a book whose depth and value are better appreciated each time one returns to it.

11. Class notes, summer 1957.

12. T. S. Eliot and George Hoellering, *The Film of Murder in the Cathedral* (London, 1952).

13. Fyodor Dostoyevsky, *Crime and Punishment*, trans. Constance Garnett (New York, 1950), p. 532.

14. C. L. Barber, "Strange Gods at T. S. Eliot's 'The Family Reunion,'" in Unger, *A Selected Critique*, p. 415.

Chapter Seven

1. Many detailed studies of the quartets have appeared, some of the best being Helen Gardner's *The Art of T. S. Eliot* (New York, 1959), Raymond Preston's *"Four Quartets" Rehearsed: A Commentary on T. S. Eliot's Cycle of Poems* (New York, 1946), and especially for exhaustive identification of sources and analyses of their relevance, Grover Smith, Jr.'s indispensable if sometimes puzzling *T. S. Eliot's Poetry and Plays: A Study in Sources and Meaning* (Chicago, 1956). Of the analyses I have read, none is better than Kenner's in *The Invisible Poet: T. S. Eliot*. An excellent brief reading is found in Smidt. Though it seems to me to go astray in some details, Smidt's account admirably and justifiably reverses the normal trend of multiplying detailed analyses until the major import of the poems is lost in a dark wood of exegesis. With Smidt's example in mind, I have tried to give a simple consecutive reading of each of the four poems in turn.

2. "Dante," *Selected Essays*, p. 229.

3. Kenner, p. 289.

4. *Poems in English, 1530-1940*, ed. David Daiches and William Charvat (New York, 1950), pp. 548-49. By permission.

5. See Unger, "T. S. Eliot's Rose Garden," *The Man in the Name*.

6. Kenner, p. 297.

7. Smith, pp. 262-63.

8. Quoted in Smith, p. 264.

9. Drew, p. 165.
10. Temple Classics, *Paradiso,* p. 405.
11. Penguin Classics, *Purgatory,* p. 271.
12. Temple Classics, *Purgatorio,* p. 319.
13. *The Song of God: Bhagavad-Gita,* trans. Swami Prabhavananda and Christopher Isherwood (New York, 1954), pp. 56-57. Quoted by permission of the Vedanta Society of Southern California.
14. *Ibid.,* pp. 74-75.
15. *Ibid.,* p. 52.
16. *Ibid.,* p. 73.
17. Gardner, p. 177.
18. *The Confidential Clerk* (New York, 1954), p. 45.
19. Temple Classics, *Paradiso,* p. 405.

Chapter Eight

1. *The Use of Poetry,* p. 153.
2. Irwin Edman, "Incantations by Eliot," *Saturday Review of Literature,* XXXIII (June 24, 1950), 56.
3. Foster Hailey, "An Interview with Mr. T. S. Eliot," *The New York Times* (April 16, 1950), II, 1, col. 5.
4. W. K. Wimsatt, "Eliot's Comedy," *Sewanee Review,* LVIII (1950), 666-78.
5. D. W. Harding, "Progression of Theme in Eliot's Modern Plays," *Kenyon Review,* XVIII (Summer, 1956), 348.
6. *On Poetry and Poets,* p. 92.
7. Jones points these out in his excellent chapter on *The Confidential Clerk.*
8. Jones analyzes *The Elder Statesman* in detail, with great understanding and sensitivity toward the relevance of its themes to the whole body of Eliot's works.
9. Sophocles, *The Theban Plays,* trans. E. F. Watling (Harmondsworth, Middlesex, 1952), p. 120.

Chapter Nine

1. *American Literature and the American Language,* p. 23.
2. *The Use of Poetry,* p. 154.
3. *American Literature and the American Language,* p. 10.
4. *The Poetry of T. S. Eliot* (London, 1932), p. 14.

Selected Bibliography

PRIMARY SOURCES

The following are listed in the order of their publication as separate works, though many of the poems and essays appeared earlier in periodicals or other people's books.

A. Poems

Prufrock and Other Observations. London: The Egoist, Ltd., 1917.
Poems. Richmond, Surrey: The Hogarth Press, 1919.
Ara Vos Prec. London: The Ovid Press, 1920; New York: Alfred A. Knopf, 1920.
The Waste Land. New York: Boni and Liveright, 1922.
Poems 1909-1925. London: Faber & Gwyer Ltd., 1925.
Journey of the Magi. London: Faber & Gwyer Ltd., 1927.
A Song for Simeon. London: Faber & Gwyer Ltd., 1928.
Animula. London: Faber & Faber Ltd., 1929.
Ash-Wednesday. London: Faber & Faber Ltd., 1930; New York: G. P. Putnam's Sons, 1930.
Marina. London: Faber & Faber Ltd., 1930.
Triumphal March. London: Faber & Faber Ltd., 1931.
Words for Music. Bryn Mawr, Pennsylvania: Bryn Mawr Press, 1935.
Two Poems. Cambridge: Cambridge University Press, 1935.
Collected Poems 1909-1935. London: Faber & Faber Ltd., 1936; New York: Harcourt, Brace and Co., 1936.
Old Possum's Book of Practical Cats. London: Faber & Faber Ltd., 1939; New York: Harcourt, Brace and Co., 1939.
East Coker. London: *The New English Weekly*, 1940; 3rd ed. London: Faber & Faber Ltd., 1940.
Burnt Norton. London: Faber & Faber Ltd., 1941.
The Dry Salvages. London: Faber & Faber Ltd., 1941.
Little Gidding. London: Faber & Faber Ltd., 1942.
Four Quartets. New York: Harcourt, Brace and Co., 1943; London: Faber & Faber Lt., 1944.
A Practical Possum. Cambridge: Harvard Printing Office and Department of Graphic Arts, 1947.
The Undergraduate Poems. Cambridge: *The Harvard Advocate*, 1949. Unauthorized reprint.
Poems Written in Early Youth. Stockholm: Privately printed, 1950.
Collected Poems of T. S. Eliot 1909-1962. New York: Harcourt, Brace & World, 1963.

Selected Bibliography

(Translation)

Anabasis: a Poem by St.-J. Perse. London: Faber & Faber Ltd., 1930; New York: Harcourt, Brace and Co., 1938; 3rd (rev. and corrected) ed., 1949.

B. *Plays*

Sweeney Agonistes: Fragments of an Aristophanic Melodrama. London: Faber & Faber Ltd., 1932.

The Rock. London: Faber & Faber Ltd., 1934; New York: Harcourt, Brace and Co., 1934.

Murder in the Cathedral. Acting ed., Canterbury: H. J. Goulden Ltd., 1935; first complete ed., London: Faber & Faber Ltd., 1935; New York: Harcourt, Brace and Co., 1935.

The Family Reunion. London: Faber & Faber Ltd., 1939; New York: Harcourt, Brace and Co., 1939.

The Cocktail Party. London: Faber & Faber Ltd., 1949; New York: Harcourt, Brace and Co., 1950.

(With George Hoellering) *The Film of* MURDER IN THE CATHEDRAL. London: Faber & Faber Ltd., 1952.

The Confidential Clerk. London: Faber & Faber Ltd., 1954; New York: Harcourt, Brace and Co., 1954.

The Elder Statesman. London: Faber & Faber Ltd., 1959; New York: Farrar Straus and Cudahy, 1959.

Collected Plays. London: Faber & Faber Ltd., 1962.

C. *Prose*

Ezra Pound, His Metric and Poetry. New York: Alfred A. Knopf, 1917.

The Sacred Wood. London: Methuen & Co. Ltd., 1920.

Homage to John Dryden. London: The Hogarth Press, 1924.

Shakespeare and the Stoicism of Seneca. London: Oxford University Press, 1927.

For Lancelot Andrewes. London: Faber & Gwyer Ltd., 1928; Garden City, N.Y.: Doubleday, Doran and Co., 1929.

Dante. London: Faber & Faber Ltd., 1929.

Thoughts After Lambeth. London: Faber & Faber Ltd., 1931.

Charles Whibley A Memoir. London: Oxford University Press, 1931.

Selected Essays 1917-1932. London: Faber & Faber Ltd., 1932, 3rd ed., 1951; New York: Harcourt, Brace and Co., 1932, new ed., 1950.

John Dryden the Poet the Dramatist the Critic. New York: Terence and Elsa Holliday, 1932.

The Use of Poetry and the Use of Criticism. London: Faber & Faber Ltd., 1933; Cambridge: Harvard University Press, 1933.

After Strange Gods: A Primer of Modern Heresy. London: Faber & Faber Ltd., 1934; New York: Harcourt Brace and Co., 1934.

Elizabethan Essays. London: Faber & Faber Ltd., 1934.

Essays Ancient and Modern. London: Faber & Faber Ltd., 1936; New York: Harcourt, Brace and Co., 1936.

The Idea of a Christian Society. London: Faber & Faber Ltd., 1939; New York: Harcourt, Brace and Co., 1940.

Points of View. London: Faber & Faber Ltd., 1941.

The Music of Poetry. Glasgow: Jackson, Son & Co., 1942.

The Classics and the Man of Letters. London, New York and Toronto: Oxford University Press, 1942.

Reunion by Destruction. London: The Pax House, 1943.

What Is a Classic? London: Faber & Faber Ltd., 1945.

Die Einheit der Europaischen Kultur. Berlin: Carl Habel Verlagsbuchhandlung, 1946.

On Poetry. Richmond, Va.: Whittet & Shepperson [printers], 1947. For Concord Academy, Concord, Mass.

Milton. London: Geoffrey Cumberledge, 1947.

A Sermon. Cambridge: University Press, 1948.

Notes Towards the Definition of Culture. London: Faber & Faber Ltd., 1948; New York: Harcourt, Brace and Co., 1949.

From Poe to Valéry. New York: Harcourt, Brace and Co., 1948.

The Aims of Poetic Drama. London: The Poets' Theatre Guild, 1949.

Poetry and Drama. Cambridge: Harvard University Press, 1951; London: Faber & Faber Ltd., 1951.

On Poetry and Poets. London: Faber & Faber Ltd., 1957; New York: Farrar Straus and Cudahy, 1957.

Knowledge and Experience in the Philosophy of F. H. Bradley. London: Faber & Faber Ltd., 1964; New York: Farrar, Straus & Co., Inc., 1964.

SECONDARY SOURCES

A. *Bibliography*

GALLUP, DONALD. *T. S. Eliot: A Bibliography Including Contributions to Periodicals and Foreign Translations*. [New York: Harcourt, Brace and Co., 1953.] Definitive to 1951.

For bibliographies of criticism of Eliot's works, see below Unger (*Selected Critique*), Jones, and Greene. See also the excellent annual bibliographies in *PMLA* and the indexes to *Abstracts of English Studies*, as well as Joseph Marshall Kuntz, ed. *Poetry Explication*, rev. ed. Denver: Swallow, 1963.

B. *Studies of Eliot by One Author*

DREW, ELIZABETH. *T. S. Eliot: The Design of His Poetry*. New York: Charles Scribner's Sons, 1949. Jungian interpretations.

GARDNER, HELEN LOUISE. *The Art of T. S. Eliot*. New York: E. P. Dutton & Co., 1959. One of the best studies of *Four Quartets*, relating them to all of Eliot's poetry. Sensitive treatment of metrics and imagery.

GREENE, E. J. H. *T. S. Eliot et la France*. Paris: Boivin, 1951. Good bibliography.

HOWARTH, HERBERT. *Some Figures Behind T. S. Eliot*. Boston: Houghton Mifflin Co., 1964. Too recent for use in this study. Appears best yet on Eliot's life and times through World War II.

JONES, DAVID E. *The Plays of T. S. Eliot*. Toronto: University of Toronto Press, 1960. Better on each play than most studies.

KENNER, HUGH. *The Invisible Poet: T. S. Eliot*. New York: McDowell Obolensky, 1959. An engaging study; one of the best.

LUCY, SEAN. *T. S. Eliot and the Idea of Tradition*. London: Cohen & West, 1960. Contains a very useful date list for Eliot's writings.

MATTHIESSEN, FRANCIS O. *The Achievement of T. S. Eliot: An Essay on the Nature of Poetry*, with a chapter on Eliot's later work by C. L. Barber, 3rd ed. New York: Oxford University Press, 1958. A penetrating study; few, if any, better.

MAXWELL, DESMOND E. S. *The Poetry of T. S. Eliot*. London: Routledge & Paul, 1952. Reprints *Doris's Dream Songs* in appendix.

SMIDT, KRISTIAN. *Poetry and Belief in the Work of T. S. Eliot*, rev. ed. New York: The Humanities Press, 1961. Especially good on early background and influences.

SMITH, CAROL H. *T. S. Eliot's Dramatic Theory and Practice*. Princeton, New Jersey: Princeton University Press, 1963. Contains perceptive, well-written studies on each of the plays.

SMITH, GROVER A., JR. *T. S. Eliot's Poetry and Plays: A Study in Sources and Meaning*. Chicago: University of Chicago Press, 1956. Indispensable. Comprehensive survey of sources and influences, plus interpretations. Often incisive, but sometimes wide of the mark.

THOMPSON, ERIC. *T. S. Eliot: The Metaphysical Perspective*. Carbondale: Southern Illinois University Press, 1963. Draws heavily on Eliot's Bradley dissertation. Abstract in orientation.

UNGER, LEONARD. *T. S. Eliot*. University of Minnesota Pamphlets on American Writers No. 8. This brief overview would be hard to improve.

WILLIAMSON, GEORGE. *A Reader's Guide to T. S. Eliot*. New York: The Noonday Press, 1957. Excellent introductory handbook to the poems.

WILLIAMSON, HUGH ROSS. *The Poetry of T. S. Eliot*. New York: Putnam's, 1933. Contains the best study of *The Waste Land* that I have read.

C. *Collections of Critiques on Eliot*

BRAYBROOKE, NEVILLE, ed. *T. S. Eliot: A Symposium for His Seventieth Birthday*. New York: Farrar, Straus and Cudahy, 1958.

KENNER, HUGH, ed. *T. S. Eliot: A Collection of Critical Essays.*
Englewood Cliffs, N.J.: Prentice-Hall, 1962. Varied viewpoints,
well selected.

MARCH, RICHARD, and M. J. TAMBIMUTTU, eds. *T. S. Eliot: A
Symposium for His Sixtieth Birthday.* Chicago: Regnery, 1949.

RAJAN, BALACHANDRA, ed. *T. S. Eliot: A Study of His Writings by
Several Hands.* London: Dennis Dobson, 1947.

UNGER, LEONARD. *T. S. Eliot: A Selected Critique.* New York:
Rinehart & Company, Inc., 1948. Contains many valuable
articles—Mr. Unger's being perhaps the best; also contains an
excellent bibliography of writings on Eliot to 1948.

WILSON, FRANK. *Six Essays on the Development of T. S. Eliot.*
London: The Fortune Press, 1948.

D. *Valuable Essays on Eliot in More General Works*

FOSTER, GENEVIEVE W. "The Archetypal Imagery of T. S. Eliot,"
PMLA, LX (1945), 567-85. Jungian interpretations, some perhaps overdrawn.

GREGORY, HORACE, and MARYA ZATURENSKA. "T. S. Eliot, the
Twentieth-Century Man of Feeling in American Poetry." *A
History of American Poetry, 1900-1940.* New York: Harcourt,
Brace and Co., 1942. Interesting 1942 summary including
predictions since fulfilled.

HOLROYD, STUART. "T. S. Eliot." *Emergence from Chaos.* New York:
Houghton Mifflin, 1957. Emphasis on spiritual biography.

LEAVIS, FRANK R. "T. S. Eliot." *New Bearings in English Poetry.*
London: Chatto and Windus, 1932. Early favorable criticism;
still of interest.

NELSON, ARMOUR H. "Critics and *The Waste Land*," *English Studies*,
XXXVI (1955), 1-15. Traces in remarkably clear but non-
interpretive fashion the range of reactions to *The Waste Land.*

PRAZ, MARIO. "T. S. Eliot and Dante." *The Flaming Heart.* Garden
City N.Y.: Doubleday & Co., 1956. Best study of Dante and
Eliot that I have found.

UNGER, LEONARD. "Laforgue, Conrad, and Eliot." *The Man in the
Name.* Minneapolis: University of Minnesota Press, 1956. A
model of appropriate practice in evaluating Eliot's borrowings.

WILSON, EDMUND. "T. S. Eliot," *Axel's Castle.* New York: Scribner's,
1931. Interesting early evaluation.

E. *Books on Eliot and Others*

MOORMAN, CHARLES. *Arthurian Triptych: Mythic Material in Charles
Williams, C. S. Lewis, and T. S. Eliot.* Berkeley: University of
California Press, 1960. Points out significant parallels.

WRIGHT, G. T. *The Poet in the Poem.* Berkeley: University of
California Press, 1960. On Eliot, Yeats, and Pound.

Index

Act, Action, 34, 36, 44, 61, 68, 75, 94, 103, 114, 120, 123-24, 126, 129, 131, 133-36, 140-42, 149, 155

Adams, Henry, The Education of, 48

Aeschylus, 44, 113-14; *Agamemnon,* 44, 113-14; *Choëphoroe,* 114; *Eumenides,* 114-15, 117-18, 128

Aiken, Conrad, 26, 27

Alain-Fournier, 24

Aldington, Richard, 29

Allusions, 6, 37

Amor, 45

Andrewes, Lancelot, 47, 71-72, 89-90

Anima, 47, 56

Annunciation, 132-33

Appleplex (*see,* Eeldrop and . . .)

Aquinas, Thomas, 61

Ariel Poems, 72, 95

Aristophanes, 100

Aristotle, 8, 26, 32-33, 49, 101, 149, 160, 174; *De anima,* 32-33, 160, 174; Katharsis, 44; *Poetics,* 149; *Metaphysics,* 174

Arjuna (*see also, Bhagavad-Gita*), 134-35, 160, 163

Arnold, Matthew, 39

Athenaeum, The, 29

Atman (*see also, Bhagavad-Gita*), 134-35, 137, 140

Auden, Wystan Hugh, 168

Baedeker guidebooks, 40, 42

Barber, C. L., 117, 178

Baudelaire, Charles, 20-21, 36, 62-63, 72, 93

Beatrice, 36, 40, 58, 70-72, 76-78, 80, 82, 85-88, 90-91, 93-94, 130, 140, 177

Beaumont, Francis, 44

Bergson, Henri, 24

Bhagavad-Gita, 35-36, 75, 114,

120, 129-30, 134-36, 140, 160, 163, 179

Bible, The, 36, 46, 47, 52, 62, 65, 69, 72-74, 79-82, 84, 89-90, 96, 100, 105, 113, 120, 126, 132

Blake, William, 32, 72

Bonagiunta of Lucca, 79

Book of Common Prayer, 73

Bradley, F. H., Preface, 24, 72

Brahman (*see, Bhagavad-Gita*)

Bramhall, Bishop John, 72

Browne, E. Martin, 104, 107, 178

Browning, Robert, 138

Brunetto Latini, 138

Buck, Philo M., *Directions in Contemporary Literature,* 57, 175

Buddha, 53, 57, 60, 151-52; "The Fire Sermon," 57, 60, 62-63, 175

Byron, George Gordon, 6th Baron, *Don Juan,* 19

Cavalcanti, Guido, 76, 86

Chapbook, The (*see, Doris's Dream Songs*)

Chorus, 102, 105-13, 115, 117

Christ, 45-47, 52-53, 58, 61, 65, 87-88, 90-91, 95-96, 111, 118, 120, 123, 125-26, 128, 130, 151-52

Christian, Christianity, 23, 45, 47, 53, 56, 58-60, 65, 71-72, 75, 84, 92, 100, 107, 110, 112, 117, 125, 128, 136, 143, 157, 159, 161, 169-70

Christian ritual and liturgy, 36, 48-49, 51, 55, 57, 61, 64, 72-74, 79-81, 84, 86-88, 90-91, 94, 126, 130

Church, the, 40, 72-74, 80, 82, 88, 94, 99, 103-5, 107-8, 110, 128, 170

Claudel, Paul, 24

Cleophas, Sister Mary, 177